Permanence in
Child Care

D1798978

The Practice of Social Work
General Editors: Bill Jordan and Jean Packman

Permanence in Child Care

June Thoburn
Anne Murdoch
Alison O'Brien

Basil Blackwell

First published 1986

Basil Blackwell Ltd
108 Cowley Road, Oxford OX4 1JF, UK

Basil Blackwell Inc.
432 Park Avenue South, Suite 1503,
New York, NY 10016, USA

British Library Cataloguing in Publication Data

Thoburn, June
    Permanence in child care.—(The Practice of social work; 15)
    1. Adoption—Great Britain   2. Foster
home care—Great Britain
I. Title   II. Murdoch, Anne   III. O'Brien
Alison   IV. Series
362.7'33'0941   HV875.7.G7
ISBN 0–631–15097–8
ISBN 0–631–15098–6 Pbk

Library of Congress Cataloging in Publication Data

Thoburn, June.
    Permanence in child care.

    (The practice of social work; 15)
    Bibliography: p.
    Includes index.
    1. Adoption—Great Britain. 2. Children, Adopted—
Great Britain. 3. Children, Adopted—Great Britain—
Family Relationships. 4. Social work with children—
Great Britain. I. Murdoch, Anne, 1953–
II. O'Brien, Alison, 1952—. III. Title.
IV. Series.
HV875.58.G7T48   1986   362.7'34'0941
ISBN 0–631–15097–8
ISBN 0–631–15098–6 (pbk.)

Typeset by Cambrian Typesetters, Frimley Surrey
Printed in Great Britain by Billings Ltd, Worcester

Contents

Preface

The fox gazed at the little prince, for a long time.
'Please – tame me!' he said.
'I want to, very much,' the little prince replied.
'But I have not much time. I have friends to discover, and
a great many things to understand.'
'One only understands the things that one tames,' said the
fox.

(Saint-Exupéry, The Little Prince*)*

The little prince had an unsatisfactory relationship with a rose whom he loved, but who was sometimes cruel to him. He set off on a tour of the universe in search of a cure for the ill-defined ache within himself. This book describes the journeys undertaken by 29 children who, with the help of their social workers, set out on a quest for permanent new parents, in the hope of filling a gap within their lives.

'Permanence' is a term which begs many questions, especially at a time when marital breakdown and 'reconstituted' families have become common. In telling the story of the first three years of The Child Wants a Home, a project which was set up by the Children's Society when enthusiasm for permanent placement for children in care was just catching on in Britain in a big way, we seek to answer some of these questions, and to raise others. In doing so, we are conscious that to aim for permanence in our society is to aim very high indeed, and we use the term as a form of shorthand for its important components – security, stability, the experience of living as a member of a family; the sense of belonging and being cared about for the foreseeable future; and, for the lucky ones, the experience of loving and being loved.

When we started our study, enthusiasm was high, and more and more older children were being adopted. In 1975, 8 per cent of children adopted by non-relatives were over the age of five, but by 1983 the proportion had risen to 26 per cent, albeit of a smaller total (down from 10,256 to 4,008). But facts and independent evaluations were in short supply. As late as 1984 the House of Commons Social Services Committee commented, 'We would favour more research into what is happening both in respect of adoption from care, and of the outcomes of adoptive placements' (DHSS, 1984).

By 1985 other independent evaluations were beginning to appear, earlier placements had stood or failed to stand the test of time, and workers were learning from their experiences and adjusting their aims and methods accordingly. In our concluding chapter we draw on this cumulative wisdom to offer our view of a 1985-model 'permanence movement', which is older and wiser than when we started, and which has learned from its mistakes but is justifiably proud of its successes.

The hardest aspect is that research is by nature always a photograph in time – the photo taken has been of our project when young, green, and well-intentioned. Already there have been many changes, but it is interesting to realize that much of the core remains today, and much of that core has been commended by the consumers. (Children's Society, 1984)

As we put the finishing touches to our book, we are aware that many more statutory and voluntary agencies are just embarking on similar enterprises. Whilst each will be different, we hope that this account will be of value to them, and thus to the children who are just setting out on their own very personal quest.

Acknowledgements

We acknowledge first and foremost the debt we owe to Elisabeth Gould, the project leader of The Child Wants a Home, and to the other members of staff, especially Marianne Halliday, Liz Jelley and Meg Newman, who were in at the start, and shared with us their failures as well as their successes, their frustrations and sad moments as well as their happier ones. The study was undertaken at their invitation, and with the full blessing and co-operation of the Children's Society head office and regional staff.

Next, and just as importantly, we thank the children in our study and their new brothers and sisters who tolerated our questions, and allowed us to monopolize their parents for hours at a time; the parents themselves, who took such trouble to try to get over to us what it was really like to go through the process of taking a child with special needs into their homes; the local authority workers who fitted us into their busy schedules and crowded offices, and shared with us their successes and their regrets; and the panel members, inquirers and others who allowed us to observe their meetings and completed our questionnaires.

During the past four years our thinking has been influenced by many social work and research colleagues. We hope they will find this book has something in it to justify the time they gave us. We single out for special thanks for their encouragement, and illuminating comments, Martin Davies, Jane Rowe, Peter Wedge and the members of the research advisory committee: Winifred Stone, Ian Sparks, Barbara Whitfield, Graham Flatt and Martin Nightingale.

Our thanks go also to our colleagues in the social work sector at the University of East Anglia and the Bethel Child and Family Centre, who have offered advice and encouragement whenever asked. Steve Mosley, Marcus Borgès and Jackie Collins provided assistance with computing, and Edna Hitchborn helped with typing. We are grateful to her and to Joan Mills, who typed the many drafts, for coping with our deadlines, and for their attention to detail.

The research would not have been possible without a grant from the Small Grants Committee of the Department of Health and Social Security, for which we express our gratitude. Our thinking about what it all means was taken forward as a result of a workshop on the subject funded by DHSS, and we are particularly grateful to Jenny Griffin of the Office of the Chief Scientist for enabling this to happen, and for her encouragement throughout. Neither the DHSS nor any of the persons mentioned here necessarily shares the views expressed in the book, for which, along with any errors, we accept responsibility.

Finally we thank John, Jim and Ian and our children for their encouragement, interest and forbearance when we arrived home late from lengthy interviews in the depths of Norfolk, or appeared annoyingly vague about matters of importance in our own family lives.

The extracts from *The Little Prince* by Antoine de Saint-Exupéry, copyright 1943 by Harcourt Brace Jovanovich Inc.; renewed 1971 by Consuelo de Saint-Exupéry, are reprinted by permission of Harcourt Brace Jovanovich Inc. and William Heinemann Limited.

June Thoburn
Anne Murdoch
Alison O'Brien

Abbreviations and Terminology

It is not easy to protect confidentiality when numbers are so small. Names have been changed and used randomly, so that individual children or adults cannot be traced. Genders have sometimes been changed, as have ages and numbers of siblings when this did not materially affect the point to be made. All the project workers with children in the study were women, and local authority workers are either male or female as the mood took us. Participants will often recognize themselves, and will sometimes recognize others. We hope that nothing will be recognizable which can do damage to delicate and continuing relationships. We have sometimes with regret had to leave out comments and incidents which would inevitably have been recognizable and could have caused offence or harm.

TERMINOLOGY

Permanence/permanent placement Used to describe a placement with a family (which may be the first family or a substitute family) which offers 'continuity of relationships with nurturing parents or caretakers and the opportunity to establish lifetime relationships' (Maluccio and Fein, 1983).

'Secure' or 'permanent' foster placement We are aware that, as the law stands, fostering is not divisible in this way. We use the term to mean a foster placement which the care authority, new parents and child intend to be a permanent placement.

Family/parent/mother/father Because most of the report is concerned with the children and their adoptive and foster families, parent and family usually refer to the new families. We use the terms 'natural parents', 'natural family' and 'birth parent' if we are referring to the family into which the child was born.

Social worker   Used if the agency by which he/she is employed is immaterial. Otherwise *project worker* and *local authority worker* are used.

ABBREVIATIONS

ARE   Adoption Resource Exchange (now the BAAF Resource Exchange)

BAAF   British Agencies for Adoption and Fostering (formerly known as ABAA, Association of British Adoption Agencies, and ABAFA, Association of British Agencies for Fostering and Adoption)

CWAH   (The) Child Wants a Home

DHSS   Department of Health and Social Security

HMSO   Her Majesty's Stationery Office

PPIAS   Parent to Parent Information on Adoption Services

1

Permanent Placement: An Overview

There is at the moment considerable confusion over the significance of the search for 'permanence' in a placement. It should not have become a synonym for adoption. The search for permanence in our view could be accomplished in many ways. . . . A placement can never be permanent because of course a child becomes an adult and makes his own life. Adoption is only one eventual outcome among many. It is, however, the most permanent possible outcome for a child unable to continue life with his natural family. . . . A trend towards more adoptions from care can be anticipated over the decade ahead, and we would welcome it. More than ever before adoption is for some children both desirable and possible. . . . We must sound some notes of warning. There is some danger that a new bandwagon is rolling connecting adoption with the idea of permanence.

(Report of the House of Commons Social Services Committee, DHSS, 1984, pp. 75–8)

These somewhat ambivalent comments by a committee of MPs that was making a thorough examination of child care services in England and Wales at the time of our study give a flavour of the debate to which this book makes a contribution. Before proceeding to a detailed analysis of the work of one permanent placement project, it is necessary to consider the state of the art of home-finding for children in long-term care before The Child Wants a Home opened its doors. This is especially so because of the very strong influence which earlier developments had on the Children's Society's policy-makers and social workers. Rowe (1983) provides an excellent short review of recent developments in fostering, and other important British studies are those of Cooper (1978), Parker (1980), Triseliotis (1980) and Smith (1984).

THE REDISCOVERY OF THE 'CHILDREN WHO WAIT'

Packman (1981) has shown how each apparently new trend in child care has its roots in an earlier period, but a convenient starting date for this brief review of the development of the 'permanence movement' (Jordan, 1981) is 1975. In that year the Children Act introduced several changes, including a number which made adoption a more likely option for some children in long-term care, and suggested custodianship as a way of achieving stability for others. (We had hoped when we designed the research that it would have been possible to consider the impact of custodianship, but it was still unimplemented when the study was completed, so we and those we interviewed were only able to speculate about what effect it might have had on some of the families in our study.) The following year saw the publication of *Foster Care: a guide to practice* (DHSS, 1976), which provides a useful indication of what was considered at that time to be good practice. In 1975 also, the Association of British Adoption Agencies added 'fostering' to its remit and title, signalling the start of the debate, which is one of the central themes of this study, about the respective roles of adoption and long-term fostering in securing continuity and a sense of belonging for children in care who cannot return to their families of origin.

Rowe and Lambert (1973) had already demonstrated that the hopes which lay behind the preventive and rehabilitative sections of the 1963 Children and Young Persons Act had been less than fully realized. Large numbers of children were still coming into care; preventive services were inadequately developed or not developed at all, so that the structural and personal problems of the families of children coming into care remained unalleviated (Holman, 1976), and chances of children returning home remained poor; and social work, especially in the early stages after reception into care, was often incompetent and insufficiently informed about the effects of separation during the early weeks and months on both children and their parents (Jenkins and Norman, 1972; Rowe and Lambert, 1973; Fanshel and Shinn, 1978; Aldgate, 1980; Thoburn, 1980; Thorpe, 1980; Rowe et al., 1984).

Two other important strands which need to be mentioned figured in the mid-seventies debate about the future directions of child care policy for the 'rediscovered' children growing up in the limbo of unplanned care, and both are in evidence in the 1975 Act. The first is the anxiety engendered by the Maria Colwell tragedy and a succession of inquiries into child abuse cases. In the absence of adequate protective resources in the community, 'play-safe' policies evolved which meant that children were at times unnecessarily received into care and stayed there too long. The second strand, in the shape of the writings of Goldstein and his colleagues (1973), came to the rescue of those who dared not return children home because they lacked the resources to ensure 'good enough' care and protection. Goldstein and his co-authors argued that those responsible for choosing the 'least detrimental alternative' placements for children in care should acknowledge that the prime need of those children was to live with parent figures with whom they could be sure they would remain. If the birth parents were unable to offer this security, then their place should be taken, within time limits appropriate to each child's age, by 'psychological parents', either foster parents with whom they were already living, or new parents willing and able to take on this role. Furthermore, in contradiction to currently held views of social work practice with foster children (Holman, 1975; DHSS, 1976), they argued that for many children contacts with birth parents tended to impede the growth of attachments and render the placement vulnerable, and so should cease. Those who were attracted by this argument found support in research studies such as that of George (1970), which showed that long-term foster homes were indeed highly vulnerable to breakdown, although no clear reasons for this were identified, and what research evidence was available tended to refute the 'one set of parents only' argument. Kelly (1981) offers a useful summary of the arguments about parental contact for children in long-term care.

The mid 1970s then, saw restatements of the aims of prevention and effective social work and foster care practice to keep separated parents and children in touch with each other; and statements about the need for permanence, preferably via adoption, for children who were unlikely within a reasonable time-span to return to their parents. Some workers and writers opted for one position or the other; the majority tried to incorporate both into their thinking about the undeniable problem of the 'children who wait' (Rowe and Lambert, 1973; Fox, 1982). The purpose of the study reported here was to focus on these statements about permanence, and specifically on the attempts of the Children's Society to translate them into practice in East Anglia.

TOWARDS A PERMANENCY POLICY FOR CHILDREN IN CARE

When children go to live with people other than their natural parents, three parties stand to gain or lose by the process: the child; the parents and extended family; and the new parents and their extended family. Increasingly in Western society, a fourth party, a voluntary or statutory social work or adoption agency, is involved, and courts give legal sanction to the arrangement and define the rights and duties of the parties. Until comparatively recently, the two major avenues for transferring the care of a child from one family to another, adoption and fostering, have been seen as different processes for different sorts of children, usually carried out by different agencies. Although the primary stated purpose of both, at least in recent times, has been to provide for the welfare of the child, they also to different extents seek to provide a service for the other parties. Parents unable or unwilling to care for children have a means whereby they can try to ensure that someone else meets their needs; families who would like a child or additional children have a means of identifying available children; and social work agencies charged with caring for children, for whatever reason, are enabled to offer them family life in a foster home, or discharge them to the care of adoptive families.

Adoption used to be seen essentially as 'a service for childless couples that gives them an opportunity to raise a child from infancy and to substitute as closely as possible for biological parents, as well as fulfilling a nurturing parental role' (Churchill, 1979, p. 9). Thus it was seen as an appropriate resource for healthy, usually white, babies, or, as there came to be a shortage of healthy babies, for young children, possibly non-white and possibly with a slight health problem. It was also laid down by law that adoption should, except in unusual and therefore rare circumstances, be available only for those children whose parents were willing for all their rights and duties to be transferred to the new parents. Children above the age of two or three whose parents no longer wished or felt able to care for them were placed by their parents with foster parents or relatives, or came into the care of state or voluntary social work agencies, the younger ones usually being placed with foster parents. Until the 1960s this was also the case for black or mixed-race children of any age, and those who had mental or physical health problems. Sometimes this arrangement lasted for a short period, but in other cases the child remained with the new parents until adulthood, sometimes with continued contact with the natural family, but more often with contact tailing off, so that the placement became a *de facto* adoptive placement. With fostering, the prime beneficiaries were usually intended to be children and parents, the foster parents offering a service to parents and child, directly or through the intermediary of a social work agency. Adoptive placements were most usually made by voluntary agencies, whilst most foster placements were arranged and supervised by state agencies. Even when statutory agencies acted as adoption agencies for babies, this service was usually operated by a separate section.

The first moves away from this rather rigid division between adoption and fostering came in Britain and the United States with the recognition that adoptive homes could be found for non-white babies, usually with white families. While adoption continued to be mainly a service for childless couples, with the babies who would otherwise have remained in care, and the natural parents who would otherwise have had to care for children whom they would have preferred to relinquish, being also beneficiaries, an element of altruism came more often into the motivation of adopting families. Increasingly those who already had children decided to enlarge their families by adoption rather than by child-bearing, so as to offer a home to a baby who might otherwise have remained in care. From then on, both in America and in Britain, the needs of children, and the altruistic motive, became more important, and the range of possibly 'adoptable' children grew, as did the range of families seeking to adopt. In both countries an alliance was formed between adoption agencies, initially in the voluntary sector, and groups of adoptive parents, who, seeing the advantages for their own adopted children, undertook to find new families for many more. In Michigan, the pioneering agency Spaulding for Children grew from the efforts of the parents' group Council on Adoptable Children, and developed methods of working which became almost a blueprint for later agencies (Donley, 1975). In Britain, the British Adoption Project's success in finding adoptive homes for non-white babies (Raynor, 1970) led in 1968 to the setting up of the Adoption Resource Exchange to link adopters and available children. At first the 'hard-to-place' deemed to need this service were all babies, but by 1978 36 of the 105 children placed were over five and many were handicapped.

As in America, adoptive parents (through the medium of Parent to Parent Information on Adoption Services) joined forces with adoption workers to set up in 1978 the first British adoption agency specializing in the placement of 'hard-to-place' children, Parents for Children (Sawbridge, 1983).

As it became increasingly common for older children to be placed for adoption, it became more likely that the children placed would be in care. In the days when it was assumed that adoption was only suitable for healthy white babies, local authority social workers had developed the practice of receiving into voluntary care non-white babies or those without a 'clean bill of health' whose parents requested adoption and were unable or unwilling to care for them. Thus the first group of children in care to benefit from broader definitions of adoptable children were those whose parents had always hoped for adoption for them, many of whom were in residential care (Tizard, 1977).

Up to this stage, such developments were widely welcomed and uncontroverisal. Apparently there were no losers from these moves, but if children in care could more easily be placed for adoption there might be a reduction of pressure to find resources for preventive health, education, income maintenance and personal social services for disadvantaged families or for families with handicapped children. An 'ambulance service' for the rescue of a small number of casualties is cheaper than a preventive service for the far greater numbers at risk, and some, most notably Holman (1976), Stevenson (1980) and Jordan (1982), urged that the gains for the small numbers of children in care who were placed for adoption should not be at the expense of those who would be vulnerable if more resources were not made available to them and to their families.

If adoption was to be considered an available option for more children in care, the next step had to be the placing of children whose parents did not request adoption, and who might actively oppose it. Such an extention of the ranks of 'adoptable' children was, and still is, highly controversial. In Britain there has always been the possibility that children in long-term foster care would be adopted by the foster parents who had cared for them, usually for several years, and it is common practice to place children 'with a view to adoption'. This usually takes place with parental consent, but there is provision for dispensing with consent, and the 1975 Act strengthened the position of foster families considering adoption. (Rowe et al., 1984, discuss these changes and describe their impact on children who had been with the same foster parents for several years, and who in some cases were adopted by those families.) Thus, although some children each year were adopted as older children, it was unusual until the late 1970s for older children to be placed directly for adoption. This step was taken in America rather earlier and more wholeheartedly, owing to a legal system which in many states allows adoption without parental consent following a court decision to terminate parental rights (Kadushin, 1970; Kadushin and Seidl, 1971). Also, long-term foster care has never become so well established in America as in Britain, and writers on foster care such as Fahlberg (1981, p. 34) stress its inability to provide stability and continuity. If children became free for adoption, they were rarely allowed to stay with their foster families and were usually placed with new families. Thus there was more discomfort about 'foster-care drift' in America, especially following the publication of *Beyond the Best Interest of the Child* (Goldstein et al., 1973; and see Sherman, 1973).

The result was that several states passed legislation which was designed to provide long-term security for children at risk, and to diminish the numbers in residential care. Such legislation usually required the state welfare services to help natural parents meet the needs of their children while they continued to live in the parental home. Failing this, the parents should be helped to resume care of the children as soon as possible. If the natural family were unable to offer a reasonable prospect of permanence, courts were empowered to free the child for adoption.

Thus by the mid 1970s several specialist voluntary and statutory agencies had been set up to provide permanence for older children in care, if necessary without the consent of the parents (Churchill, 1979). It is interesting to note, however, that the objective of several of these agencies was to provide permanence not simply by adoption. Lahti (1982) describes the work of a special unit in Oregon which aimed to secure permanence for 259 children under the age of 12 who had been in care for a year, and were considered by their caretakers as not likely to return home, and as adoptable. Three years later they had placed 66 per cent of these children in permanent homes, but, interestingly, for 26 per cent 'permanence' meant returning to natural parents. 20 per cent were adopted by their foster parents and 20 per cent by new parents. Thus, although much of the pioneering work in America to provide a secure home for 'hard-to-place' children was undertaken by adoption agencies, others, with small caseloads and a high level of commitment, used new techniques in the search for a wider range of permanency options (Jones et al., 1976; Stein et al., 1978; Maluccio and Sinanoglu, 1981; Lahti, 1982; Fein et al., 1983).

Although the 1975 Children Act offered encouragement and a degree of legal protection to long-term foster parents who might want to adopt their foster children, and promised 'custodianship' for those who wished to put their fostering on a more secure legal footing, it did not alter the basic permise that parental consent should normally be required before a child could be adopted, even when parental rights were held by a local authority. However, social workers who were already convinced by the arguments of Goldstein and his colleagues (1973) were impressed by evidence from America that permanent homes *could* be found. At this stage it was the success in finding adoptive families which was most widely reported. Preventive work had had its day following the 1963 Act, and had been judged to be less than successful; and, for many of the children needing a secure family placement, attempts at long-term foster care, had proved unsuccessful.

In the late seventies in a series of articles (Adcock and Lawrence, 1975; ABAFA, 1977; Bacon and Rowe, 1978), the lack of adequate planning for children in care was explored, and courses and training packs were put together to help improve the situation. Several local authorities undertook surveys of the children in their care and identified those in need of permanent placement. A major theme was the questioning of the widely held view that continued parental contact for children, including those likely to remain in long-term care, was usually beneficial. Holman's (1975) article in which he categorized foster homes as 'exclusive' or 'inclusive' summarizes this debate, as does Rowe's (1977) article on the place of fostering in social work. There was complete agreement about the need to make every effort to return children home and to help parents meet their children's needs and offer them security. However there were sharp differences about the efforts to be made to secure a child's proper development if such steps failed, especially if parents or child wished to remain in contact. Those stressing permanence as the primary aim pointed to the evidence of foster home breakdowns, and suggested that continued parental contact could, as the work of Goldstein and others had suggested, be one of the factors associated with breakdown. Tizard (1977) argued strongly that new families need to be totally in control of the way they bring up their children before they will fully commit themselves to them. Thus a model of child care social work was advocated which broke with what was previously advocated as good practice (DHSS, 1976). Social workers should make every effort to return children to their parents as quickly as possible, but parents who were reluctant to resume care of their children should not be pressed to do so, and the advantages of adoption for the child and for themselves should be pointed out to them. Plans for children in care should be explicit and should be agreed by a more senior member of staff. A time limit appropriate to the age of the child should be agreed, after which a decision should be made to seek a permanent placement, preferably with an adoptive family. It was to be hoped that the parents, having been given every assistance to resume care, would agree that it was in their child's interests to have a secure future with a new family. In a few cases it would be in the child's interests to remain in contact with the natural parents or with other relatives, and the possibility of adoption with continued contact (subsequently referred to as 'open adoption') was introduced. Where children were not placed directly for adoption, parental rights would be assumed for those in voluntary care; and, when a child was being prepared for and placed with a new family, the chances of a successful placement would often be improved if there were no contact with the natural parents. It was essential for senior management to sanction such plans in order to ensure that they did not change, as had so often happened, when there was a change of social worker. Despite critical comment from some social workers and pressure groups (Jordan, 1981; Kelly, 1981), this model of practice was adopted by several local authorities and by individual social workers in others. Some social services departments set up their own home-finding units, but most relied heavily on the voluntary agencies, which, as noted earlier, were already developing skills in the placement of 'hard-to-place' children. Most were adoption agencies, and, although they might in some cases initially place under foster care legislation, their aim was usually adoption. A few, such as the Thomas Coram Foundation, the Children's Society, Barnardo's Cambridge Cottage Project (Fratter et al., 1982), and some of the special units within local authorities, sought to achieve permanence by placing children either with adoptive families or in long-term foster homes, seeking to ensure the maximum permanence the law could afford.

Other agencies heeded the message about lack of planning and the need to offer security, but retained their belief in the value of continued parental involvement in the lives of most children in long-term care. The National Foster Care Association played an increasingly important role in the efforts to improve foster care and social work practice, as did groups such as The Voice of the Child in Care (James, 1980), the Family Rights Group (1982), Harlow Parents' Aid and the British Association of Social Workers (1982). Despite the attempts of the such bodies to restate the value of foster care, the possibility or desirability of offering the advantages of permanence by means of 'secure' long-term fostering was seriously questioned, to the extent that some were saying that it should never be a placement of first choice (Hussell and Monaghan, 1982).

PERMANENT PLACEMENT: THE NUTS AND BOLTS

The terms 'permanence' and 'permanent family placement' present some problems, partly because of the impermanence of family life for increasing numbers of children whose parents separate (Lambert and Streather, 1980), and partly because whether these terms are seen as 'good' or 'bad' depends on where one stands in the spectrum of opinion about child placement policy. Thus Jordan (1981) has written in negative terms of the 'permanence movement', and Rowe has talked about 'the unacceptable face of permanence' (quoted in Fitzgerald, 1982, p. 5). The term 'permanent family placement' is used in the present study as a shorthand way of describing placement with a family – usually, in our context, not the birth family – as a result of which children experience stability, security and a sense of belonging, in confidence that their needs will be met by parents who genuinely care for them as individuals, and with whom, barring unforeseen accidents, they will remain until they are adults – or longer, if they wish or need to. The legal status, whether they are fostered or adopted, is significant in our terms only in so far as it detracts from or contributes to the ability of the placement to meet their needs, in the eyes of either the children themselves or members of their new families.

The first British agency to move wholeheartedly into the

placement of older children was the Independent Adoption Agency, which in 1972 began to work closely with a London borough to provide adoptive homes for 'hard-to-place' children in care (James, 1980). In 1976 Parents for Children set out to place for adoption handicapped children living in the Greater London area, and in the same year Barnardo's New Families Project opened its doors in Glasgow. At about the same time the Family Care Adoption Agency in Edinburgh and the Thomas Coram Foundation started to work in similar ways. In 1978 Barnardo's opened its 'adoption shop' in Colchester, and that unit now works in close partnership with other family-finding units of Essex County Council (Wedge, 1986). Barnardo's has since opened similar units throughout the country, and most other national and regional adoption agencies have moved, at least partly, in this direction.

Essential to the development of these new enterprises was the Adoption Resource Exchange, or BAAF Resource Exchange, as it is now known. A child and family 'clearing house', it started in 1968 with 20 member agencies and in that year facilitated the placement of eight children. By 1982–3 the total annual number of placements had reached 236 and there were 174 member agencies (128 local authority and 48 voluntary agencies). With its foundation the ARE opened up an important channel for realizing the aspirations of the small band of converts to the permanence movement for small but growing numbers of children in care. We use this spiritual terminology advisedly, as no one who had contact with workers in this field in the late seventies could fail to notice the elements of faith and mission in their work. Indeed, the word 'mission' was used by more than one of the specialist workers we interviewed.

By the late seventies a number of local authorities, most notably Lothian and Lambeth (McKay, 1980; Hussell and Monaghan, 1982), had begun to identify those children in their care who were in need of permanent family placement. Such a policy was often accompanied by decisions to close residential child care units. Sometimes the children were further classified into those needing an adoptive family and those needing long-term 'secure' foster care. To give an example, one of the larger local authorities that made use of the services of The Child Wants a Home identified approximately 230 children in care (mostly in residential care but some in foster homes) who needed new family placements. This was approximately 20 per cent of the children in care. Of these, 60 were assessed as needing a family who could take them on an indeterminate basis, and 169 as needing permanent placement. For 55 of the 169, adoptive homes were felt to be appropriate, whilst 114 were said to need 'secure' foster placements.

Faced with such information, and with the accounts from America and increasingly from British voluntary agencies of the experimental and time-consuming methods which seemed to be necessary in placing older children, these local authorities had to decide on appropriate policies. In the course of our study we interviewed several managers from different authorities who were responsible for deciding how the work should be organized. Some, usually those with fewer children in care, chose to make no organizational changes other than carefully to monitor review decisions in order to discourage 'drift', and to encourage all workers to rethink their methods of working to achieve permanent placement. Most of the authorities that were committed to a permanency policy were members of the ARE and would refer some children for adoption either through the ARE or directly through one of the voluntary agencies, such as Parents for Children.

Some authorities set up their units to locate permanent homes, sometimes seeking adoptive homes only, sometimes making 'secure' long-term foster placements, and sometimes also running treatment or 'professional' schemes for 'hard-to-place' children (usually teenagers) where permanence was not the prime aim (Cooper, 1978; Hazel, 1981; Shaw and Hipgrave, 1983). Wedge (1986), in describing the Essex Social Services Department home-finding units, has discussed the organisational problems of introducing a specialist home-finding service. Even those authorities setting up their own permanent placement teams found in the late seventies that they needed to use the ARE and voluntary agencies, if only to 'clear a backlog'. The voluntary agencies, for their part, also needed the ARE. They were mostly small, and often operated within relatively small geographical areas. Although some children were referred directly by neighbouring authorities, for effective operation they needed the wider source of referrals which the ARE could provide. Also, 'special needs' children required a wider choice of potential new parents, and potential new parents needed a wider range of children to choose from. The voluntary agencies were dependent for their survival on a fee for service, the fee being paid by the agency placing a child. (This is contrary to the practice which often operates with baby adoption, where *families* adopting a child are asked to make a 'donation' to cover the operating costs of the agency.) The ARE, in providing a mechanism for a steady flow of referrals to the smaller voluntary agencies, was an important element in ensuring that they were able to operate at all.

In 1980 the ARE published *Working Together: a guide to the policy, procedures and practice of inter-agency adoption placements*. As Sawbridge (1980, p. 170) has pointed out, the 'aim of the Adoption Resource Exchange was not simply to achieve the family placement of children who otherwise were being kept waiting, but also to improve standards of practice by enabling agencies to work together, to trust each other, and to learn from each other'. The Exchange also helped to negotiate a scale of charges for inter-agency work, which is regularly updated. The ARE guidelines were to be followed by all using the Exchange, but they were also used widely in other inter-agency adoption and fostering work. In 1980 the BAAF started the 'Be My Parent' scheme – a photo-listing service for children who are especially difficult to place, and this booklet can now be seen by potential adopters in 355 locations throughout Britain. A similar service is offered by the PPIAS newletter, which features children in need of new families and is also widely available. As with the ARE, these two schemes have been important to the growth of the small voluntary agencies, as they have helped to bring home to potential adopters the real needs of real children. The increased use of television and local and national press has had a similar effect.

SUMMARY

In this chapter we have noted the following trends:

- towards permanent placement for children who had been in care for several years;
- towards adoption for groups of children who had not previously been considered 'adoptable';
- towards the closure of residential units for children;
- towards earlier decision-making once a child has come into care;
- towards increased willingness to dispense with parental consent to adoption, and to terminate parental contact;

– towards the consolidation of systems, making it easier to bring together new parents and children from different parts of the country.

These trends were conducive to the growth of small voluntary agencies such as the CWAH. Staff from these agencies enthusiastically spread the message about their successes and their methods, became increasingly involved in training local authority workers and offering assessment and consultancy services, and in some cases moved into social services departments to set up 'permanency' units there.

2

The
Research Study

David's recent years had been traumatic and grave consideration had to be given as to whether it was fair to deliberately expose him to more questioning. However, it was possible that our experiences, both good and bad, would possibly benefit other families as they worked towards successful adoptions so we felt morally bound to agree. . . . As the research study continued over a long period we became quite used to our lady interviewers and totally at ease with them. They were neutral and after a year or so of social workers representing someone in particular, it was at times a relief to talk to them. They somehow just became part of our life at that time.

(Adoptive mother writing 'after the event', Children's Society, 1984)

Some families never mentioned the research, others burbled cheerfully about what they said and what was said to them. Two families told me being questioned made them re-think their position (an example of research affecting a situation). Two children told me they disliked the psychological tests, feeling they were 'thick' and had failed. . . . Mostly I felt the researchers were on a neutral track as far as interpretation was concerned, but once I sensed personal bias and I feel it is still there in the findings on that same issue. When the findings were due, I felt as sick and as nervous as if waiting for an important exam result.

(CWAH project leader, Children's Society, 1984)

THE THEORETICAL FRAMEWORK

In 1979, when the Children's Society was planning its new unit in Norwich, permanent family placement of 'special needs' children in Britain was still essentially experimental, numbers placed were small and placements still tended to be short, so that the growing belief in the possibility and desirability of permanent family placement for such children was based mostly on 'in house' reports of small numbers of fairly recent placements and on the enthusiasm of the workers involved. The Society, recognizing this, invited us to monitor the work of the project and to undertake an independent evaluation of the early placements made.

THE SAMPLE

Negotiating access was fairly straightforward, as we had the enthusiastic co-operation of the Society and of the CWAH workers. Families offering to take a child were told of the research soon after they contacted the agency, and requests to take part were sent as soon as they were approved by the Adoption Panel. How far this acted as a 'carrot' we cannot be sure, but in the event only one of the first 15 families with whom children were placed declined to be interviewed. Statistical data and material from the files and interviews with social workers are included, so that, for purposes of numerical analysis, this is a total sample of the children referred in the first three years.

Children were approached through their local authority social workers and in only the one case mentioned above was permission to interview the child refused. Each of the local authority social workers for the first 29 children referred agreed to be interviewed, as did most of the previous foster parents or residential workers. Older children were asked if they were willing to talk to the researchers and the psychologist. All agreed to take part, but it is doubtful, given the power relationships, if they saw this as a completely free choice. The new families of six children placed by the Society before the project started and some of their children agreed to 'pilot' the guided interview schedules. The main study comprised 21 children placed with 15 new families between July 1980 and July 1982 (the case study group); and the 'withdrawn' group of eight children referred during this period but not placed.

Seven of these children were introduced to new families but not placed with them, and we interviewed four of the children and six of the families concerned.

THE INTERVIEWS

The older children and each of their new parents, as well as some new siblings, were interviewed separately in their own home, and, as each visit involved two researchers, different family members could be interviewed simultaneously. Interviews took place just after placement, at the one-year stage, and 18 months to two years after placement. Some families were also interviewed just before placement. Interviews lasted at least 90 minutes. (In most cases, interviewing marriage partners separately at least once proved useful, as differences in their perceptions sometimes appeared more marked than when they were interviewed jointly.) When interviewing children (usually in the kitchen, with plenty of biscuits to hand) it was particularly helpful to have a second researcher talking to parents in a separate room.

All the local authority and project social workers (except for one from Scotland) were interviewed in their offices either before or as soon as possible after the placements had been made. In addition, CWAH workers were interviewed at the two-year post-placement stage and the local authority workers for the children withdrawn from the project were contacted by telephone and completed a postal questionnaire about each child's progress.

All interviews were tape-recorded and notes made on a precoded interview schedule. Initial interviews with children, families and agency social workers were unstructured; all other interviews were semi-structured, using multi-choice, precoded schedules.

INTERVIEWING CHILDREN

We interviewed all except one of the children in the study group who were over the age of eight years, on the assumption that children younger than eight (and most of the children in this study were below average for their age in mental development) would not be able to formalize their thoughts in such a manner as to cope with a structured interview. However, even those under eight were quite experienced interviewees. Most had been in care for a major part of their lives and therefore regularly engaged in interviews with their social workers and other caring adults. Thus, whilst we did not formally interview these youngsters, we did meet and talk to them informally on a number of occasions and observed them with members of their new families. During her sessions with the children before placement and at the two-year stage, the psychologist in the research team assessed their development, using a variety of tests to establish the children's perception of their social worlds, and asking questions about prominent persons in their lives. In addition, their general chatter was tape-recorded during the psychologist's interviews. In the course of the two years, several children did 'life story work' with their new parents or social workers and were willing to share the contents of their books with us.

Our approach to interviewing the older children was similar to that used in interviewing adults, except that the sessions varied from 30 minutes with the under tens and educationally handicapped children to 90 minutes with two teenagers. Whilst it is important to be kind and understanding to child interviewees, it is equally important not to be condescending. The teenagers in particular responded positively to a mature approach and wanted to help other children in care by sharing their thoughts and experiences.

A note of caution should be introduced here. Children in particular are sensitive to messages which interviewers unwittingly communicate to them and we were concerned that they might have slanted their replies according to their perceptions of us. In addition, it was necessary to explain fully to parents and children at the first meeting that we were independent researchers, in no way connected with the work of the CWAH or the local authorities, and that their detailed comments would only be shared amongst the researchers. Most children seemed reassured by this, and some were very open with us. In other cases it seemed that we were no more to be trusted than any of the other adults who had tried to enter their private worlds. Experience has also shown that probing questions may produce unnatural or untruthful answers, because children feel they must produce a particular response, or any response at all which will get the interviewer to move to the next question. There were distinct advantages in seeing most of them at different times and in different settings, sometimes alone, sometimes with their new parents or brothers and sisters, or in social gatherings arranged by the agency. We got to know each other better and we believe that the interpretations of our data are more reliable as a result.

The desirability of interviewing children on more than one occasion was made evident in analysis of interview responses. Attitudes change over time, and children are possibly more influenced by events and preoccupations of the moment than adults. Rich (1968) has described the pitfalls encountered when interviewing children, and we encountered most of them. Interviewers can often be rude or discourteous to children without realizing it, and the child will respond to this. Some children, on the other hand, may be antagonistic towards males or females and this may be transferred onto the interviewer. Some children may even have a 'dependent hostile relationship' with adults in general – depend on them but hate this dependency. Teenagers often become hostile when they are shy and defensive; others completely 'clam up'. Some children like to test adults to their limits, and the interview situation is no exception. In addition, if children feel forced into the interview they may protest against this in their behaviour, and some made it clear to us that they would prefer to be elsewhere.

QUESTIONNAIRES

Postal questionnaires were used as a method for collecting data from both families and social workers who were not part of or associated with the case study group. Each questionnaire included precoded multi-choice responses and open-ended questions as well as asking for specific details about respondents, and was sent with a stamped addressed envelope.

Questionnaires were sent to all those who over a two-and-a-half-year period had made inquiries about becoming long-term foster or adoptive parents and had attended at least one open meeting. This questionnaire was designed to provide information about the sorts of people who offered a home to a 'special needs' child; about their reasons for doing so; and about their perceptions of the work of the agency.

The response to the inquirers questionnaire was 65.2 per cent (75 out of 115). It is likely that those not responding included a higher proportion of inquirers who had attended only an open meeting and were therefore less likely to be motivated to complete a questionnaire. 13 of the 14 local authority social workers for children referred but not placed, or placed after July 1982, completed a postal questionnaire which was designed to find out their perceptions of the work of the agency and the outcome for those children not placed.

DIRECT OBSERVATION

We have been involved in two types of observation: casual observation of people in their everyday environment – social workers in their offices and families in their homes; and more structured observation of specific events, such as preparation groups and panel, team and planning meetings, where the participants' approval was, where possible, gained before we started observing.

In the final phase some of these meetings were used as opportunities to feed back tentative conclusions, so that staff members had the chance to comment on our interpretations and we could check on aspects about which we were not clear. This book owes much to the constructively critical exchanges with individual participants and with groups of staff which took place at this stage.

PSYCHOLOGICAL ASSESSMENT AND EVALUATION OF
CHILDREN'S PROGRESS

There are many problems associated with evaluation, some of which were made more manageable by our involvement with the project before the children were placed. In particular this allowed the psychologist to assess all except one of the study children and three of the 'withdrawn' children before or very shortly after placement, and 20 of the 21 children placed at the 18-month to two-year stage. The aim was to measure the children's progress after placement, and also to compare their well-being before placement and approximately two years after placement, with that of peers with any similar disabilities. In this research 'well-being' is used as a global term to refer to the child's general health, appearance, behaviour, social competence and self-esteem.

In addition to the psychological assessment of the children, Rutter forms A(2) for parents and B(2) for teachers (Rutter, 1975) were completed. Form A was sent to the previous caretakers of those children referred who were in the appropriate age group, and then to the new parents of 20 of the study children at the two-year stage; and form B to the teachers of children after they had been placed in their new families for 18 months. Used in conjunction with the psychologist's reports, the Rutter forms provided useful measures of well-being, highlighted changes in the children's behaviour over time and proved to be a helpful indication of their relationships with significant others. They also allowed us to compare the children in the study with other samples of children with whom the Rutter questionnaires have been used.

A 100 per cent response rate was achieved from parents and teachers asked to complete Rutter forms. The forms were scored for anti-social behaviour and neuroticism, and general comparisons were made between scores at the pre-placement stage and scores two years after placement. Another measure of the children's well-being at the two-year stage was derived from CWAH social workers for the case study children and from local authority social workers for the 'withdrawn' group. The workers were asked to state, first, how they perceived the child's current well-being as compared with that of others in the same class at school or, in the case of the younger handicapped children, other handicapped children in their age group; and, secondly, how the child's general well-being had changed for better or worse in the last two years.

Information and opinions about well-being were, then, collected from new families, the children themselves, the agency and local authority social workers, medical and psychological reports on files, Rutter forms completed by parents and teachers, psychological tests, and direct observations by psychologist and researchers. Inevitably there were some cases where the evidence was in conflict. In such cases the research team of psychologist, teacher and social worker, all of whom had seen all except one of the study children at least once, sifted through the evidence and came to an agreed conclusion about well-being and progress since placement, attachment to parent figures and likely permanence of placement.

THE ADVANTAGES AND DISADVANTAGES OF SMALL-SCALE QUALITATIVE RESEARCH

Whatever the methods used, ethical and professional questions must be answered. In small-scale research where it is possible that individuals are vulnerable or that respondents' reputations are at stake, such issues are paramount and indeed in many ways highlight both the strengths and weaknesses of this model of research. Some important questions are

- to whose needs and interests does the research respond?
- how are conflicts between the needs of policy-makers and the needs of participants to be resolved?
- do the data belong to the researchers, the participants or the sponsors?
- what is the status of the researchers' interpretations relative to those of others?
- what can be said about the 'objectivity' of researchers who bring to the research their own distinct perceptions of the subject and who almost inevitably come to care about the parents, children and workers they get to know over the period of study?
- what is the 'true' picture when respondents change their opinions over time; when the working methods change, in the light of experience; and when all parties have 'hidden agendas' at a time of transition, and are liable to use research interviews to help them work on their mixed feelings about the powerful and important people in their lives? (For discussions of 'consumer research' in the personal social services, see Shaw, 1975; Barclay Committee, 1982.)
- with such small numbers, how is the promise of confidentiality to be honoured if the final report is to be other than a series of uncorroborated statements or bland generalizations?
- how is the knowledge gained in the research to be disseminated, and what weight can be placed on the findings, given the small numbers invovled?

We do not pretend to give satisfactory answers to each of these questions, but offer the following 'advantages' of our choice of methods. A small-scale study is a powerful vehicle for collecting information and opinions, and for understanding and communicating complex situations. It provides an opportunity to explain what is there by building on the detailed study of situations or cases. In our small-scale research, the data pool is deep rather than wide, and the aim is to illuminate the unique, rather than the representative, case. This makes it a particularly appropriate method for our study, where each child and each family is more than usually 'unique'. Moreover, the total 'pool' of 'special needs' placements in Britain is not wide as yet. To forgo the opportunity of studying these early placements in depth, and waiting until enough children have been in placement for long enough to justify a large-scale quantitative study, would be to do a disservice to all the children placed in the meantime. The task of this book is for the researchers to interpret, and the readers to weigh up for themselves, how the unique experiences of these families and social workers, and their own attempts to make sense of them and generalize from them, can be used to the advantage of other families about to embark on similar but equally unique adventures.

SUMMARY

The work of The Child Wants a Home during its first three years was described and evaluated. The first 29 children referred were followed through from the initial inquiry to two years after placement with new families or withdrawal from the project. The chapters which follow comprise a case study of the project and case studies of the 29 children, 21 of whom were placed, with 15 new families. In addition, questionnaire responses from 75 of the 115 applicants to foster or adopt who attended open meetings are analysed.

A wide range of methods was used to capture the complexities of social and professional behaviour and interaction. These included direct observations, field notes, tape-recorded guided interviews, questionnaires and standardized tests. A variety of sources of 'evidence' was used to assess the success of each placement and the progress made by the children since placement or withdrawal. The work of the project itself was evaluated by comparing its achievements at the three-year stage with its aims as expressed to the researchers and in publicity material before it opened its doors.

3

The Child Wants a Home: Development, Description and Evaluation

> I can't speak too highly of their efficiency and co-operation, and their explaining at each stage what they were going to do – what the plan was. They have been very patient. I have learned so much about how to do it.
>
> *(Local authority worker)*

Voluntary agencies have always played an important part in the provision of social services for children, originally by being the major providers, and more recently by setting up pioneering projects. They are still the major providers of adoption services, especially for babies, although, following the implementation of the 1975 Children Act, local authorities are required to take major responsibility for adoption work. Most of the voluntary agencies have their origins in a religious body, although one of the pioneer agencies in this field, the Independent Adoption Agency, started life as the Agnostics Adoption Society. Three large national voluntary child care agencies, Dr Barnardo's, the Children's Society and the National Children' Home, have for several years been setting up innovative projects in the fields of preventive work with families and communities, residential care and family placement. They have, however, become increasingly dependent on income from statutory sources, either through grant aid or through fees for services. As the statutory authorities have taken on more responsibilities, voluntary agencies have had to negotiate their role, not only nationally, but also with individual local authorities. Holman (1981, 1983) and Phelan (1983) have described the Children's Society's innovative projects in the area of community social work and family centres, and Fitzgerald and his colleagues (1982) have written about its first venture into the field of permanent family placement for older children in care, this first project being a development of the Society's traditional role of providing residential care. The Child Wants a Home also grew out of a long-established role, in this case the provision of an adoption service for the eastern counties of England, which had for several years been finding homes for babies with 'special needs'.

Having become convinced by the work in America and Britain and by their own experience of working with children in care that there was a need for a permanent placement agency in the Norwich area, managers from the Society's regional office met with managers of the East Anglian social services departments. Responses ranged from enthusiastic to lukewarm. Had the project needed to rely solely on local authorities for referrals, a more whole-hearted response would have been needed, but the existence of the ARE and the fact that the Society was already carrying out an adoption and fostering role in the region meant that it was not dependent on full local authority backing before deciding to go ahead. It may be that the wish to keep up momentum by going ahead without total support from all the local agencies led to some lack of warmth in the early stages, and to fewer direct referrals from some of them than had been hoped for.

A terraced house near the centre of Norwich was purchased; booklets outlining the aims and methods of the agency, the types of children to be placed and the methods of referral were printed and circulated to all social workers in three local authorities; a project leader, an existing Society social worker who had strongly supported the development, two social workers and a secretary were appointed; and in April 1980 The Child Wants a Home opened its doors.

THE AIMS OF THE PROJECT

From discussions with the project leader and other social workers and reference to publicity, we identified the following aims against which the work of the project could subsequently be measured.

The prime aim was to provide permanent homes for children in care who were likely to be hard to place. In the introductory leaflet the 'target group' of children was defined as physically and mentally handicapped children of all ages; sibling groups; school-age children and teenagers. The second aim was to provide permanent homes directly to some of those children in the care of East Anglian authorities who might otherwise be less satisfactorily placed in residential care or in less secure fostering situations, or might be 'drifting' in an unplanned way between home and care or between different placements. Thirdly, in so doing, the project aimed to influence the placement policies and social work practice of local agencies, and of other agencies referring children, so that practices conducive to permanence might benefit larger numbers of children in care. A fourth aim was to try out new methods of working. More specifically, it was hoped that the definition of a fairly small geographical area would allow for the greater use of group work at all stages of the process. The fifth aim was to raise consciousness about the plight of children in care and to provide information on children needing permanent families to people in the area who might be able to offer them a home; and, finally, the project sought to place children with married couples or single people who were unable to have a child of their own, or wished to add to their families by adopting or fostering a hard-to-place child, and to try to ensure that this was a rewarding and positive experience for all members of the new families.

FINDING AND APPROVING FAMILIES

The methods employed by the agency will be discussed in detail in chapters 8 and 9, but a brief outline is appropriate here. The role of the BAAF in suggesting methods of working and in running training courses and conferences has already been mentioned. By the time the CWAH opened, there was a blueprint which followed closely the practice of American agencies (Donley, 1975; Jewett, 1978; Churchill, 1979) and was being pioneered in Britain by Parents for Children, and Barnardo's New Families Projects in Glasgow and Colchester. Like other agencies, the CWAH put the emphasis on finding families for children rather than on placing children with would-be parents. Thus the basic plan was to recruit and prepare only families who wished to, and could realistically expect to be able to, provide a permanent home for a child who had special needs. Parents for Children only approves families with a specific child in mind, and therefore keeps no 'bank' of approved families. Because the CWAH intended to work through the ARE, families had to be approved by the adoption panel before their details could be channelled into the Exchange. This meant that the agency approved families for a type of child, rather than for a named child. Whilst it was still likely that the social workers and adoption panel would have an important part to play in deciding whether a given family and child should be brought together, this was not always the case. It was possible for an approved family to take a child who was featured in the media by contacting the local authority directly and for the local authority and new parents to decide to go ahead against the better judgement of the CWAH worker or panel. Because of these indirect placements the CWAH needed to be slightly more cautious in its procedures for approving families than is the case for Parents for Children and some American agencies, who can be more confident that a child will only be placed with an approved family if the worker and panel as well as the family are convinced of the parents' ability to meet the needs of that particular child. Nevertheless, the CWAH was more adventurous and imaginative than are most local authorities and adoption agencies when deciding how to recruit families and whether to encourage them to pursue their interest. There were few ground rules of the sort usually associated with adoption, regarding the age, income, health and marital status of couples. However, the Children's Society stipulates that, if a couple are living together, they must have been married for two years, even though single men or women can apply if they do not live with a partner of the opposite sex. Also applicants must agree to help any child placed with them to grow within the Christian faith (this is referred to in the procedures manual as 'the pilgrimage concept'). A religious adviser is appointed to the panel to advise on this issue.

The project used a variety of 'hard sell' approaches to attract families, including television, radio and newspaper articles about individual children. It was recognized that the first contact of potential new parents with the agency was crucially important in encouraging them to pursue the matter, and great care was taken to be encouraging when answering telephone or personal inquirers and to provide them with appropriate information. Those approaching the project usually attended an inquirers' open meeting, where they were given more information about the sort of children for whom homes were sought, and looked at the 'Be My Parent' book, the PPIAS newsletter and wall posters showing children who had been directly referred. They were also told how the agency worked, and invited to attend a preparation group. Preparation groups, usually consisting of four or five couples or single people, met on about four occasions; inquirers were given more information and invited to think about the ways in which taking a hard-to-place child into their homes might change their lives for the better or worse. At the end of the group, families were asked to take time to think about what they had learned, and then, if they wished to apply formally for a child to be placed with them, to write to the agency giving some idea of the sort of 'special needs' child who might fit into their home. Although some applicants were interested in becoming long-term foster parents, all were treated as potential adopters. A home study was undertaken by one of the social workers, references were taken up and applicants had a medical examination. At each stage along the way, families dropped out as they realized that it was inappropriate for them to proceed. Others were 'counselled out' – that is, they were advised that their application was unlikely to be successful, or were given that impression less directly. Figure 3.1 shows the application cycle. Less than 3 per cent of inquirers eventually took a child into their homes – a figure similar to that for Parents for Children (Reich and Lewis, 1986).

All applicants to adopt a child had by law to be approved by a case committee, in this case known as the adoption panel. The Adoption Agencies Regulations (1984) have since changed the role of the panel to an advisory rather than a decision-making one, but the panel still makes recommendations about each application and each placement.

Once families were approved, there was no commitment, as there is with baby adoption, to place a child. Approval was usually with a particular sort of child in mind, and often limitations about the sort of child or the number of children were written into the approval at the panel meeting. The worker who did the home study kept in touch with the family, helping to clarify ideas and discussing individual children on direct referral to the agency, or in the Be My Parent or PPIAS photo-listings. If there was no immediate likelihood of a child being placed by the CWAH, details of approved families were registered with the ARE. Despite the name 'The Child Wants a Home', once a family had been approved it was more likely that the potential new parents would choose a child from one of the above sources than that the child, or, to be more precise, a social worker acting on a child's behalf, would choose them. Indeed several of the families in our

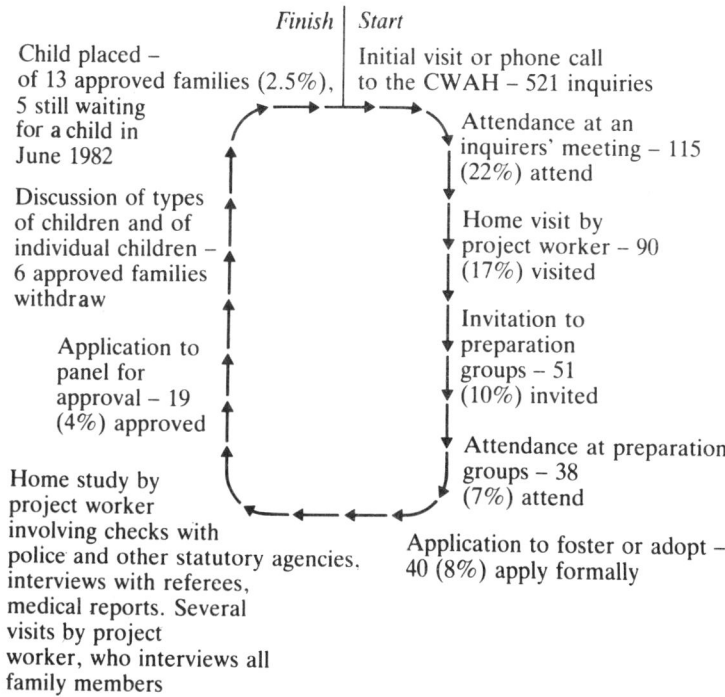

Finish | *Start*

Child placed –
of 13 approved families (2.5%),
5 still waiting
for a child in
June 1982

Discussion of types
of children and of
individual children –
6 approved families
withdraw

Application to
panel for
approval – 19
(4%) approved

Home study by
project worker
involving checks with
police and other statutory agencies,
interviews with referees,
medical reports. Several
visits by project
worker, who interviews all
family members

Initial visit or phone call
to the CWAH – 521 inquiries

Attendance at an
inquirers' meeting – 115
(22%) attend

Home visit by
project worker – 90
(17%) visited

Invitation to
preparation
groups – 51
(10%) invited

Attendance at preparation
groups – 38
(7%) attend

Application to foster or adopt –
40 (8%) apply formally

Figure 3.1 The application cycle (data for the period July 1980 to June 1982)

study had their hopes set on a particular child, perhaps featured in a newspaper or on television, before they approached the agency.

REFERRAL AND PREPARATION OF CHILDREN

Some of the children to be placed were referred directly to the project. In other cases an approved family offered a home to a child listed in one of the photo-listing services or featured in national publicity. Social workers seeking permanent homes for children usually prepared the children for placement themselves, and decided what sort of placement was likely to meet their needs: fostering or adoption; with or without contact with the natural family; near or far from where they then lived; and, within fairly broad limits, the sort of family where they were likely to feel at home. They usually completed a detailed application form; checked on the legal position, especially if adoption seemed preferable to fostering and the parents were not willing to consent; and worked with the parents and other members of the natural family with the aim of reaching agreement about the future role they might play in the child's life. Sometimes even at this stage the parents and social workers decided that return home was the best move. Sometimes parental contact was terminated, a step usually decided during a statutory review and supported by senior management. *The Code of Practice on Access* (DHSS, 1983) has since tightened up on this procedure. It might be decided that a current foster placement should be recognized as a permanent placement, following which steps would be taken to make the position for child and family as secure as possible, or foster parents might decide to apply to adopt the child. Sometimes the social workers looked for an adoptive or 'secure' long-term foster placement amongst the authority's approved adopters and foster parents, and sometimes they referred the child to the appropriate senior member of staff, usually the adoptions officer, for placement either by a specialist unit of that authority or by another agency. If the child was referred to the ARE, one of the six social workers who ran the day-to-day work of the Exchange would pick out any approved families who seemed likely to meet the child's needs, or decide to list the child's details in the 'Be My Parent' book. Details of potentially suitable approved adopters would be sent to the local authority, and the local authority social worker would contact the agency which had approved the adopters with information about the child. Sometimes more than one family was visited by the social worker, though more usually a choice between competing families was made 'on paper' by the local authority's home-finding or adoption panel as a result of discussions between social workers. At that stage the potential new parents were given details and either decided they were interested enough to meet the child or that they would prefer to wait for a youngster who seemed more suitable. Figure 3.2 summarizes the child's somewhat tortuous route to a new home.

In the early months there were several direct referrals to the CWAH, and the workers took responsibility for preparing those children for placement. This was partly because they had the time, and partly because the local authority workers lacked either the time or the expertise to do life story and other necessary work.

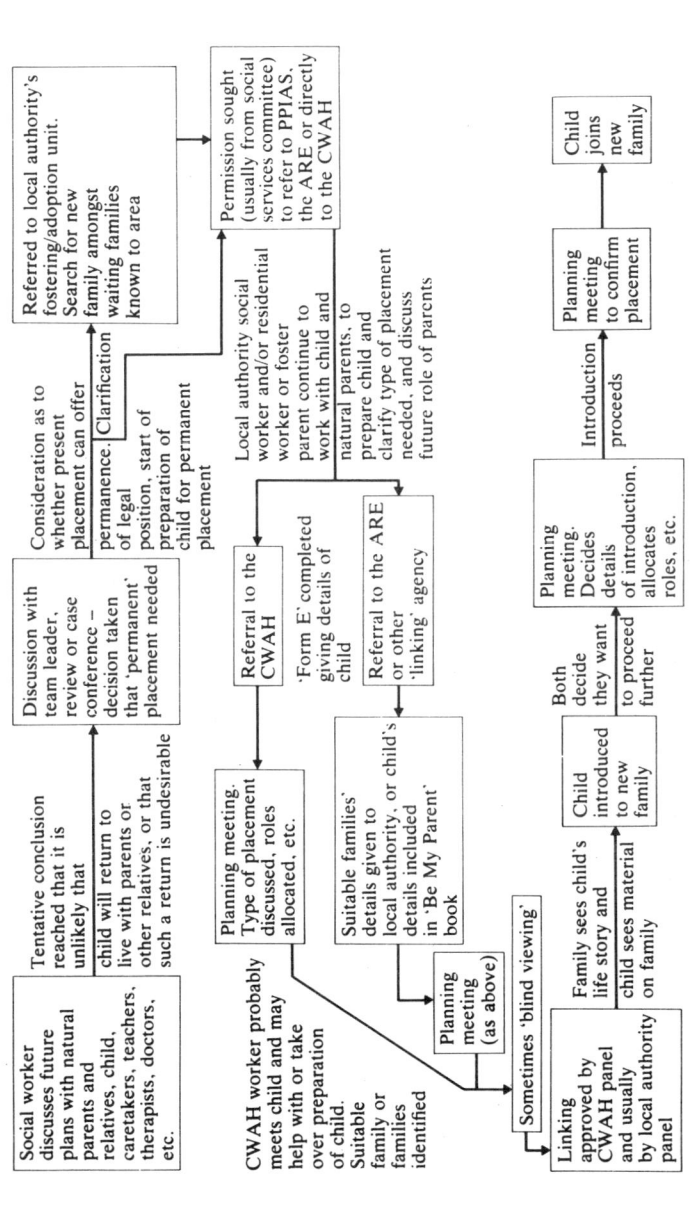

Figure 3.2 *The child's route to permanent placement*

Once a child was referred directly, or an ARE linking proposed, a planning meeting was held to decide the respective roles of the different workers and agencies and to agree a contract for the payment of the inter-agency fee. In 1980 the recommended fee was £2,095 per child placed (£3,585 in 1985), half to be paid at the time of placement and the rest at the time of the adoption order or six months after placement. If the local authority requested the agency to supervise a foster placement after 12 months, a fee of £5 per family per week was charged. (In 1985 this was £448 per child per annum.) If the placement broke down before adoption, the fee paid was not refunded. On the other hand, if the project failed to place a child on direct referral, the Children's Society received no recompense for the often substantial time spent on the case. This was also the case with indirect referrals which came to nothing.

Once it had been decided that a child and family should be introduced, arrangements to effect this were carefully worked out and the proposed linking was submitted for approval to the CWAH panel and usually also the panel of the child's local authority. Sometimes a 'blind viewing' (an opportunity for the parents to see the children without their knowing about it) was arranged, to help the family make a decision about whether to go ahead without risking an unnecessary rejection for them. Once the linking had been approved, a further planning meeting took place to decide on the process of introduction, allocate roles, and agree about whether the placement should be directly for adoption under adoption legislation, for fostering with a view to adoption in the near future once the child had settled, or for 'secure' fostering, without a decision at this stage about adoption. Agreement was reached about the level of foster payments and other financial help, such as with adaptations to the house for a handicapped child, or payment of legal fees if an adoption was likely to be contested. The local authority worker usually visited once or twice after placement, but the project took over responsibility for supervision, and after these early visits the child's worker usually came only for the purpose of the statutory six-monthly reviews.

THE PROJECT WORKERS

During the period of the research there were four social workers employed on the project, three women and one man. All were qualified, and their ages ranged from the middle thirties to early fifties. They had between seven and 13 years' experience in social work; all had previously worked for local authority social service departments, and all had wide experience of work in other social work settings. Two had children of their own and two did not. The fact that all four social workers had their desks in the same upstairs room facilitated consultation and mutual support. On the same floor was a kitchen and a comfortable room for meetings, while the secretaries and an interview room were downstairs. The four secretaries employed by the project during the research period (there was one change of part-time secretary) played a significant part in the work of the agency. Besides their secretarial, clerical, administrative and 'committee' skills, they brought to the project experience of working in settings for disturbed children – a psychiatric hospital, the probation service and the courts.

Whole-day staff meetings were held weekly, and these served several purposes: exchange of information; professional develop-ment; discussions about future plans and policy; sharing of difficulties and anxieties; and detailed discussion of cases and recommendations to be made to the panel. There was also a generous allowance of time for training, which usually involved meeting other workers from specialist placement agencies around the country. These meetings were often organized by the BAAF, whose conferences were greatly valued. The project workers identified more with colleagues from other specialist placement units than with colleagues on the staff of the Children's Society, who had a wider child care brief including preventive family social work and residential care. This is significant in considering how the ideology and practice of the unit developed over time. At least initially, all the workers strongly identified with the permanence philosophy outined in chapter one, and this was reinforced by contact with like-minded workers from other agencies. In the early days of the project they followed very closely the 'blueprint' for permanence outlined earlier, and there was a tendency to stereotype and scapegoat social workers who were not 'of the same faith'. Thus, when there was a difference of opinion between one of the workers and a local authority worker referring a child, a somewhat disparaging tone was used to describe that worker as 'a typical blood-tie social worker, from a typical blood-tie agency', and foster parents who were reluctant to proceed quickly to adopting the child placed with them were described as 'typical local authority foster parents', again somewhat disparagingly. With increasing self-confidence, the project workers developed their own distinctive styles and interpretations of permanence, and became more likely to adapt the 'blueprint' to the needs of the children and families with whom they were working.

This is particularly relevant to a consideration of one of the questions which we were interested in studying – that of the respective advantages and disadvantages of adoption and 'secure' fostering, with or without contact with members of the birth family, in providing for the long-term needs of children in care. The CWAH differed from some of the other early projects in being both an adoption *and* a fostering agency. The introductory booklet stated that the project 'specialises in finding adoptive or foster families for children who need permanent substitute care. We do not help with short-term fostering or with children who may be restored to natural parents in the future' (CWAH, 1980). It was not alone in this, but was to some extent swimming against the tide of those who considered that long-term fostering should rarely if ever be a placement of choice for children needing permanent placements. This view was expressed by a local authority adoption specialist whom we interviewed: 'We have our fostering needs. But I see them [the CWAH] as providing adoption. I can't cope with the fact that one can talk about "permanent" fostering.' The very strong influence of specialists who believed that permanence was best achieved by an end to parental contact followed by place-ment for adoption helps to explain why, despite its stated aim of providing fostering as well as adoption placements, the CWAH func-tioned, at least in its early stages, very much as an adoption agency.

A general practitioner, a child psychiatrist, a psychiatrist specializing in mental handicap, and a solicitor were available for professional consultation. In addition to advising on the cases of individual families and children, they assisted in staff development and policy formation.

THE ADOPTION PANEL

In 1980 the adoption panel, which had by law to approve all adopters and the placement of all children, had seven members. The Children's Society's regulations required that some members should possess professional expertise in an aspect of adoption and that others should be interested members of the community. The panel met fortnightly for approximately an hour, to consider applications from families wishing to adopt, and to decide what sort of child should be placed with those whom they approved; to decide whether the placement of a specific child with a particular family should go ahead; to receive progress reports on children not yet adopted; and to decide whether families wishing to adopt a child placed with them as a foster child should proceed with their applications.

The role of the panel had been worked out for baby adoptions, and its place in the adoption of older children was problematic, as is the role of any group of community representatives, such as local councillors or management committees of voluntary bodies, elected or appointed to check on and validate the work of professionals. It was further confused in this case because members had the duty to make decisions, were forbidden to meet the people affected by those decisions, and had no managerial or policy-making role in relation to the social workers on whose work they were dependent in order to make effective decisions. Whilst these complications are present with baby adoption, they are compounded when one considers the role of the panel in the adoption of older children, where 'chemistry' has, as we shall see later, as important a role to play as objective assessments of whether a couple would be 'suitable' or 'unsuitable' parents. With baby adoption the panel merely has to decide whether a couple are likely to be able to raise a child successfully. With 'special needs' children, especially if they are beyond infancy, the 'chemistry' of the relationships between specific family members and a specific child, taking into account their personalities, likes, dislikes and prejudices, has to be considered. Written reports might convey all the information needed in the case of a baby, but it is questionable whether they can do so when older children are to be placed. From observing panel meetings and discussions with workers and panel members, we concluded that in all but a small minority of the cases the major decisions were taken by the social workers. In the early stages they decided who to encourage and who to discourage, or they 'counselled families out', so that their application did not go before the panel. (We had evidence of this from our postal questionnaire to inquirers.) Most importantly, they decided what to put in their reports and what recommendations to make.

This is not to say that the panel does not play an important and necessary role, but rather to stress that it is not as straightforward as it seems, and that not to acknowledge this may lead to frustration. The panel was especially valuable if social workers could not agree; if the family could not accept the worker's view that they were not suitable; or if there was a particular ethical or controversial principle involved where the view of members of the community would be of great importance. For the workers, the fact that they were able to say to a family that, although they would recommend them, they would not make the final decision was welcome as reducing tension in what was inevitably a stressful situation – the decision about whether or not a child should be placed with people whom they had grown to like and who had shared intimate details of their family lives with them. Similarly, the knowledge that caring and informed members of the public and professional community had enough confidence to back their decisions gave the workers the confidence to take the risks which are inevitable in specialist adoption. Thus the panel validated the work of the project. In order to do so, members needed to have confidence in the work carried out, and perhaps their major role was to check on the thoroughness of the work. This they did most scrupulously, asking social workers to go back for more information on some points; and probing when there were ambiguities in reports. Sometimes they would have liked to tell the workers how they would like something done, but their lack of any managerial or policy-making role made this inappropriate, and this was a source of frustration to some members.

The role of the panel has been examined in some detail because this is perhaps the only legacy from baby adoption which seems to have been taken over without sufficient questioning of its relevance to the new style of adoption. We have already noted that the 1984 Adoption Agencies Regulations made important changes in the role of the panel, and in particular gave it an advisory rather than decision-making role, a change which is in line with our conclusions.

Despite what could have been serious causes of frustration and conflict, we found that the commitment of workers and panel members to the success of the project meant that in relation to the agency the panel fulfilled both a significant supportive role, by reducing stress and acting as a sounding board, and a valuable consultative role. The views of one panel member summarize this:

We are very much at the mercy of smoothly written but misleading reports, though poor reports invite probes about the basic quality of the fieldwork. However, I think that in our situation there is increasing recognition that this is less of an us and them situation, more a joint endeavour towards a quality service.

THE COSTS

In subsequent chapters we shall look at the financial and emotional costs to new families and the social workers. It is appropriate here to attempt to assess the financial costs, to both the Children's Society and the local authorities, of permanent placement through the use of a specialist voluntary agency. In the first three years, 30 children were placed. It is not possible to work out precisely the cost per child placed, as some work during this period was undertaken with three families with whom children were placed before the agency started and still supervised as foster children at the end of the study, and when the study ended some families were still being vetted and some who had been approved had not yet had children placed with them. However, this is to some extent offset by the fact that work had already been done on approving some families before the project started. By dividing the costs by the number of children placed we arrived at a rough average cost for the work of the project of £6,228 per child placed (about £7,300 at 1985 prices). Thus, by deducing the fee income, we estimated the average cost to the Children's Society for each child placed at £4,111. If one includes the project leader, each worker placed between three and four children each year.

These figures only include the work undertaken by the CWAH, and the actual cost is considerably greater. By adding boarding-out allowances paid prior to adoption at the rate of the average county, and the fees paid to the BAAF in respect of children referred through that agency, we arrive at an average cost per child placed of £8,189 (approximately £8,600 at 1985 prices). This takes no account of the quite considerable work of local authority social workers, managers and administrators; legal costs; enhanced boarding-out allowances, which were sometimes paid in cases of special difficulty; grants for equipment or the building of extensions; travel costs for new families at the introduction stage; and travel costs for local authority workers. Again, the estimated average cost conceals considerable variations. The least expensive placement would be that of a handicapped baby placed directly for adoption, whilst the most expensive, both because of the social work time involved and the continued payment of boarding-out allowances, would be the secure foster placement of a teenager with behaviour difficulties. It is likely that the CWAH's costs are higher than those of adoption agencies, because it has included 'secure' fostering in its remit and placed a higher proportion of older children and sibling groups who are particularly difficult to place and require extra support once placed.

Though somewhat unsophisticated, these costings are sufficiently accurate to convey the message that permanent placement, especially for older children in care, is not a cheap option. Some local authority workers told us that agency policy was for referrals to be made to specialist agencies only if all their own efforts had failed, as the fee charged was considered to be too high. Our figures show that, on the contrary, it nowhere near covered the cost. One of the agencies referring to the project estimated an average cost of about £7,000 per annum to keep a child in a residential unit. Since this cost would recur if the child remained there until leaving care, it is clear that referral to a voluntary agency, and subsequent placement, of a child in residential care would represent a considerable saving even if fostering fees continued to be paid.

If, however, the comparison is with a long-term or adoptive placement made by the agency's own staff, the balance sheet is likely to be more even. Those local authorities which have established specialist home-finding units are likely to spend as much or more, given the Children's Society subsidy of about £4,000 per child placed. Wedge (1986), researching the Essex family-finding units, found the cost per child placed slightly lower, probably reflecting less time spent on inter-agency co-ordination and travel. The workers at the Cambridge Cottage Project also place more children each year, but considerable time is saved by having all the children under one roof (Fratter et al., 1982). Local authorities which continue to see permanent placement for 'special needs' children in care as a task to be absorbed by area team workers as part of their busy caseloads are probably doing the job more cheaply. However, we would question whether they do it as effectively. Recent breakdown rates for long-term foster and adoptive placements for 'special needs' and older children are not available, but research findings on foster care suggest a higher rate of disruption within two years than in our case study (5 per cent of placements disrupted). Rowe (1983) estimates it at between 20 and 40 per cent.

EVALUATION

Before moving on to a detailed study of the children, the new families and the social work service, we summarize here our conclusions on the effectiveness of the agency as measured against the aims initially identified.

The paramount aim was to find secure family placements for children in care, and to place as many children as possible. In that 30 children were placed within the first three years, we can say that this aim was achieved. Our more detailed findings on the first 21 children show that within two years of placement only one child had to be removed from the family he had been placed with, and he was satisfactorily placed with another family and was still there two years later. This shows a 'success' rate, measured in terms of breakdown of placement within the first two years, of 95 per cent. Although, as we shall see in chapter 5, there were still important question marks over the well-being of many of the children, and it was considered that some were unlikely to become permanently attached to their new families, we considered that all except three (86 per cent of the children placed) had found a home until they reached independence.

As yet there are few British studies with which to compare the agency's work, and in any case the time scale for assessing success of placements is still short. Nevertheless, this low rate of breakdown and high assessment of success is impressive. What we do not know is whether it represents a too cautious policy, and whether, if more risks had been taken, more children would have been placed. We have no way of telling, for instance, whether perseverence with some of the placements where introductions were terminated would have paid off. Nor do we know whether some of the applicants who were 'counselled out' could have succeeded. We do not know, either, whether the rate of ten children placed a year for the first three years is a reasonable output for the size of staff. We can say that they are extremely busy, and that their careful attention to detail is seen by those who refer children as one of the reasons for their success. We should agree with this view, and stress that the complexities of inter-agency work mean that efficient and speedy communication, and determination to get the details right, are essential.

When we compare the children successfully placed with the 'target' groups identified in the publicity material, we find that children from all the groups mentioned were placed. We consider in some detail in chapter 4 the backgrounds of the children, and our findings show that the majority were hard to place because of their unhappy early lives, both in and out of care. Many of the children were indeed, as Rowe and Lambert (1973) put it, 'children who wait'.

Other aims involved the provision of 'secure' family placements for children from East Anglia and further afield who might otherwise be allowed to 'drift' in unplanned care. It was hoped that success in finding families, placing children and supporting the new families would encourage local authorities to refer more children for permanent placement or to set up their own permanent placement units. The 'target' groups included not only children who had been in care for some time, but also children coming into care for whom adoption would not have been considered in the past – for instance, handicapped babies, and older children who had been in care for only a short period but for whom a return home was considered unlikely or undesirable. Such children would be likely still to be in contact with members of their natural families, and the natural parents would be more likely to contest adoption or oppose the termination of contact. One of our hypotheses, supported by project workers in early discussions, was that a wide range of 'secure' placements, and especially placements with foster or adoptive parents who could facilitate continued contact with members of the natural family, would encourage the referral of children who needed a permanent new family but still valued contact with the 'old' one and would be unwilling to opt for a new family if it meant totally severing old ties. Such children *were* referred, and some were successfully placed. However, half the children who were not placed came into this group, and in several cases where continued contact was considered desirable, it either lapsed or was terminated before the two-year stage. In some cases this was because the referring agency asked for a placement without contact, or took the decision to terminate contact before referral, so that the CWAH workers felt obliged to go along with this decision, at least until the child's attitude showed that it had been inappropriate. However, we observed that, despite the attitude clearly expressed in the introductory brochure, the agency, at least in its early days, was not altogether happy about referrals for placements with continued parental contact. As one project worker put it, 'We call ourselves an adoption and fostering centre. But a lot of these kids really want the security of adoption. With long-term open-ended fostering there is still this fear that they will be moved.'

In our observation of open meetings and preparation groups, we saw little indication that the project was setting out to attract families who wanted to offer secure foster or adoptive homes but recognised that their role in meeting the children's needs might include helping them to stay in contact with members of the natural family. That this form of placement was made available to several of the children was due as much to the insistence and perseverance of the children and the new parents as to that of the project workers. In the early days the latter accepted referrals for secure family placements with contact, but sometimes tried to persuade those referring that contact really should be terminated. Referring to one case, a local authority worker commented, 'I think I would have considered fostering to be sufficient. I don't think it would have been helpful for him for us to terminate contact – though that is effectively what we did.'

Later, as some placements with contact seemed to be working quite well, and as, with the increasing tendency to refer children earlier in their care careers, more of the younger children referred needed to stay in contact at least with siblings, project workers gained more self-confidence in this form of placement. At the end of the research period we found considerable ambivalence still. On the one hand there was talk of the agency having a role in accepting direct referrals of more complex cases where there was, as one worker put it, 'a proper greyness rather than just woolly thinking', and where all the issues about contact and the legal situation were not fully clear. On the other hand, a worker said, towards the end of the study, 'This is primarily an adoption door. We have got firmer in moving towards adoption.' The role of the project is in any case not entirely in the hands of the Children's Society but depends also on the local authority referrers. As one worker said, 'The problem of a secondary agency is that you are beholden to the people who are using your agency. You lose children who you hve worked with because the agency decided to withdraw them, and parents you have approved get pinched by other agencies. You do a lot of work you are not paid for.'

Numbers referred directly by authorities in the area were disappointing, and by the end of the project most referrals came via the ARE. However, by the end of the study most local authorities in the region had identified children in residential care needing secure family placements, although in most cases the split between adoption units and long-term fostering remained. The major influences on local authorities were the BAAF and its publications, and the cost-saving implications of closing residential units. However, it seems likely that the existence of two specialist units in East Anglia did have an influence on local authority practice, and we found evidence that the 'training' aim was being achieved. One local authority worker commented, 'When you are working for a local authority, you can get bogged down in the bureaucracy. They [the specialist units] are more imaginative. They can take risks. I learned a lot from the way they work.'

A further aim of the project was to develop new ways of working, especially group work with children and new parents. In chapter 9 we described a 'house style' of social work support to the new families which the families found helpful, and which differed in important respects from 'traditional' social work support to foster families. Groups were used extensively at the preparation stage, and there was an annual picnic for new families, but parents showed no interest in formal groups for post-placement support.

The extent to which the project succeeded in its aim of making available to people living in the area information about children in need of permanent homes is not clear from the study, as we did not undertake any surveys of the general population. However, we can say that, of the 521 people who made inquiries, some at least would have shared with others the information they received. Also, a welcoming agency in a central location where people can go for information and to look at the 'Be My Parent' book and PPIAS newsletter is valued by organizations such as the Citizens' Advice Bureau who might not otherwise know where to refer potential adopters of children with special needs.

Finally, an aim which we noted the workers tended to play down was that of providing a service to those who wished to start or enlarge their families by providing secure foster or adoptive homes to children in need. As noted above, information was made widely available. 21 families took adoptive or foster children during the first three years, and more were approved and hoping for placements. The question of whether the agency was providing families for children, as its name suggests, or children for families, is an important and complex one to which we return in chapters 6 and 7. In an attempt to assess whose need the placement or proposed placement met, we concluded that the child's need was paramount with seven families (eight children – six placed and two withdrawn); that the balance of need was about equal in eight placements (ten children, all in the satisfactorily placed group); and that the needs of the new families took precedence in seven cases (11 children – five successfully placed and six withdrawn).

SUMMARY

In this chapter we have described and evaluated the work of the project as measured against its aims. We have also considered the cost in financial terms. In the chapters which follow, and especially in chapters 7 and 8, we consider the human costs and find that, for children, new families and social workers, the risks inolved in this work heightened the rewards, but brought sadness and sometimes anger, guilt and recriminations when they did not pay off.

Our main conclusion is that in its first three years The Child Wants a Home was an efficient and effective project, and it is important that our detailed findings should not be allowed to conceal this essentially postivie appraisal. When consumers are impressed by a service, they tend to say so in similar and rather global terms. Critical comments, however, tend to be more varied and, if they are to be useful indicators of desirable changes, need to be reported in more detail. Because of this, there is a risk that the reader of the more detailed chapters may take from our study a more negative picture than we should wish to convey. Placing our general conclusions on effectiveness early in the book will, we hope, redress the balance, though the reader will need to look in the chapters which follow for the evidence on which our evaluation is based.

4

The Children at the Time of Referral

I wanted a brother, but he wasn't the right kind of brother. After I got there I liked it but there was always a possibility in my mind I might have to leave. I said to my social worker, 'now I don't want you to get upset about this, but I would rather leave to save my brother getting hurt'. It was all anger, I was cheeky to all of them. I felt sad. There never seemed to be a quiet moment in my life. There was always an interruption. I felt sad. I never got to talk to Philip about why we got mad with each other. I say to myself, why did I do that thing. When I'm adopted, I won't have to bother about the other mum and dad.

(Eric, aged eight)

THE LEAD-UP TO REFERRAL

The 29 children in the main sample included 17 boys and 12 girls. All except one were in care at the time of referral. The exception was a physically handicapped boy whose mother had recently died, and where arrangements with relatives and friends were breaking down. For 16 of the children, the care episode which led to referral for a permanent placement was the only time they had come into care; for five, it was the second time; for seven, the third; and, for one child, the fourth. Whilst, as one would expect, there was a tendency for the older children to have had more admissions to care (seven of the 23 children aged over five at referral had at least two previous admissions), 12 of the children aged over five at referral had come into care on only this one occasion, and one of the three children under five at referral was in care for the third time. Nine of the children were under three years of age at the start of the care episode which led to the request for permanent placement; four were aged between three and five; 15 were aged between five and 11, and one was aged 12. Table 4.1 demonstrates the change in placement policy, in that it shows that some children were referred for permanent placement after they had been in care for several years, whilst some children coming into care more recently, including older children, were referred for placement within a matter of months.

Table 4.1 Age of children on coming into care compared with length of time in care at referral

| Age on coming into care (yrs) | Time in care at referral | | | | | | |
	0–6 mths	6 mths– 1 yr	2–3 yrs	4–5 yrs	6–8 yrs	9 + yrs	Total
0–2	1	2	1	0	0	5	9
3–4	0	0	2	1	1	0	4
5–11	1	2	2	4	1	5	15
12+	0	0	1	0	0	0	1
Total	2	4	6	5	2	10	29

Reasons for coming into care included request for adoption of an illegitimate child, and in seven cases the mental illness of a parent. In eight cases a 'temporary crisis' led to care, and 16 children came into care because of abuse or neglect. In fact, 19 of the children had been abused or neglected at some stage (65 per cent). 23 children came into care as a result of care orders, and three were the subject of parental rights resolutions. Only three were in 'voluntary' care.

As mentioned earlier, one of the aims of the agency was to find secure placements for children who in the past had remained in unplanned long-term care, often subject to frequent moves, or, in the case of extended stays in residential care, to frequent changes of caretaker. In order to compare our sample with a group of children in long-term care who had found permanence via the more traditional route of long-term foster placement, we looked to a sample of 105 children in the study by Rowe and her colleagues (1984, p. 12). 16 per cent of that sample, compared with only 3 per cent of the children we studied, came into care because of illegitimacy, with the mother requesting adoption, whilst 55 per cent of our sample and only 31 per cent of Rowe's were in care because of abuse or neglect.

It would seem from this comparison that there are indeed some important differences between the two groups. The children in Rowe's study were younger at reception into care (99 per cent under five at last admission to care, compared with 45 per cent of the children in this study). The children in our study differ also from those placed more recently by Parents for Children, far more of whom came into care as babies, by the voluntary route, and had no contact with natural families (Reich and Lewis, 1986). This lends support to our hypothesis that a wider range of children will be referred to an adoption and fostering unit. In our sample the reasons for admission of children placed were rather different from those of children withdrawn, in that only one of the eight who were not placed came into care because of a temporary crisis, and half of them, as compared with three of the children placed, came into care because of rejection by the natural parents. Five of the seven children who were rejected by their parents had behaviour difficulties, though whether the rejection led to the behaviour difficulties or *vice versa* it is difficult to say. The parents of three of these five continued to care for other children. The other two children who were rejected were the two Down's syndrome babies.

The main placement prior to referral for 13 children was foster care; 15 were mainly in residential care, including two at boarding school, and one was mainly cared for by relatives. However, these figures conceal the fact that all except seven of the 29 had had more than one placement during the last care episode. 14 had had between two and three placements, and eight had had four or more. Added to this, some of the children experiencing changes in placement had also been in care on previous occasions. (Four of the children who had had four placements during this care episode had been in care on two previous occasions.) Not surprisingly, the longer children had been in care, the more likely they were to have experienced changes in placement. It tends to be assumed that, if children have more than one placement in care, this is the result of bad planning or no planning on the part of social workers rather than bad luck. We therefore looked in some detail at these placements to see which was the case. For 16 of the children, including five who had been in care for at least nine years, this was the first attempt at finding a permanent substitute family. However, for 13 a previous 'permanent' placement had been made. Two had been placed for adoption, and of these one had actually been adopted previously and had had a further adoptive placement which had been unsuccessful. Five had had two previous placements which were planned to be permanent. We found that serious attempts had been made at rehabilitation in about half the cases, and 14 children had been placed back home with their parents (12 of those actually placed and two in the 'withdrawn' group). For only three of the 17 children who had been in care for over three years had there been no previous attempt at achieving permanence, either by returning a child home and offering support to the family, or by placing with a permanent substitute family. Four of the other six children where there had been no previous attempt at permanence either through rehabilitation or through substitute family placement had been in care for less than a year, and the other two for less than three years. Most of these children, therefore, would seem to be victims not so much of 'drift' as of bad luck, inadequate practice, inappropriate planning or changes in fashion. (It was once considered good practice, and still is by some, to keep siblings together in residential care, where they can more easily remain in touch with members of their birth families. (See Berridge, 1985.) We concluded that either 'drift' has been over-emphasized, or that our sample was biased in this respect, perhaps because, as we shall see in chapter 8, most of these children had had the same social worker for several years, and their workers were likely to be qualified and to see themselves as child care specialists. It should also be said that, although referral for some children after so many years was motivated by increased confidence in the possibility of successful family placement for older children, for eight children, the referral coincided with plans to close the children's homes in which they lived. This could be seen as the main reason for referral for the four children who were long-term residents, but the four others had been placed in a home to prepare another attempt at permanence following the breakdown of a previous placement.

Before moving on to a description of the children at the time of referral, we give a few details of their natural families and discuss those families' relationships with the children in care and their attitudes towards permanent substitute family placement. 23 of the children were born into working-class families, and the parents of six were lower middle class. Several of the children came into care at the time of, or shortly after, the break-up of their parents' marriage. By the time of referral, the parents of only five of the children were still living together. In seven cases the parents were separated and living alone. In nine cases one parent was married to or living with another partner, and in two cases both parents were remarried or cohabiting. In two cases the mother was dead and the father had another partner, and in two cases the children were illegitimate and the mothers were still living alone. This picture both in terms of social class and marital status is consistent with other studies of children in care (Millham et al., 1986; Packman et al., 1986).

For the children in our study, parental incapacity was less frequently a reason for admission to care than for the children in the study by Rowe and her colleagues (1984). The referral forms varied in the amount of detail they gave on the natural parents, but on the whole they were inadequate as a major source of information, for the new parents and the children as they grew up. In fact, much more was known by project workers, and local authority workers, but it was often inadequately recorded on the CWAH files. In only three cases was physical or mental incapacity of the parents a reason why they could not care for the child, and in another case low intelligence of both parents was a contributing factor. Although in two cases the mother had died, in both there was a father who was not prevented by any disability from caring. One or both parents of nine other children were described as having personality or mental health problems, but in most cases this did not stop them caring for other children, and in fact the parents of 14 children were caring for full or half siblings, or had cared for siblings who were now grown up. The plan was to place 14 children with brothers or sisters, but nine of these had other siblings from whom they were or would be separated. Five were to be placed separately from other siblings in care, and six of those to be placed on their own had brothers or sisters living with natural parents. Only three were only children. Where the plan was for children to be placed away from siblings, this was usually because the others were settled either at home or in another placement.

Most studies of children in care have noted the high probability that, if they stay in care beyond six months and especially beyond two years, they are likely not to be visited by their natural parents (Rowe and Lambert, 1973; Aldgate, 1980; Thorpe, 1980; Rowe et al., 1984). In this respect, our findings differed from those of other researchers. Thorpe (1980) found that only 27 per cent of 121 children aged five or older who had been in care for at least a year were visited by a parent. In our sample all except seven had met at least one parent during the year prior to referral, and two of these were in contact with natural siblings placed elsewhere. 17 were in contact with their mother, seven with their father, three with adult relatives and three with siblings living elsewhere. For five, contact occurred weekly; for seven, monthly; for five, approximately every two months; and, for seven, three times a year or less. This amount of contact explains why some of the children were in care for so long before attempts were made to find permanent substitute families. In other cases it is explained by the trend to earlier decision-making, since the earlier decisions are made to look for a permanent family, the more likely it is that children will still be in contact with their natural parents. In three cases social workers considered that the contact was harmful to the child; in six cases they thought it made no difference; and in 15 they considered contact with members of the natural family to be helpful. Sometimes this was because a parent was co-operating with the social worker to help the child accept the need to move to a permanent family, or because contact was helpful in reaching a decision that rehabilitation could not be achieved. In most cases it was considered to he helpful because the parent or other relative was still a significant person for the child, even though the social worker, though not always the parents or the child, had come to the conclusion that a permanent substitute home was needed. At the time of referral, social workers considered that, if a permanent placement could be found which would enable contact to continue, this would be desirable for 13 of the children (11 with parents and siblings and in three cases with siblings only).

For those cases where the social worker did not consider continued contact to be desirable after placement, a decision had to be made about whether and when contact should be terminated. In nine cases contact was ended against the wishes of at least one parent, either by the local authority or, in one case, by the matrimonial court. With five children contact was not terminated before placement but was not encouraged, and in three cases parental contact was encouraged after placement. For five other children, contact with relatives or siblings was encouraged after placement. It should be said that, for four of the children, contact was either terminated or allowed to lapse against their own wishes, and all were eventually withdrawn. In other cases children reluctantly accepted the loss of contact with their natural parents as a necessary prerequisite of finding a new family. A residential worker noted of one case, 'Pat [aged nine] used to cry in bed for her mother.' In ten cases parents agreed to adoption without contact, in one case to long-term fostering without contact, and in two cases the parents were missing. However, in nine cases parents agreed to adoption (two cases) or 'permanent' fostering (seven cases) but requested continued contact. In relation to one mother asking for continued contact a social worker said, 'His mother agreed to publicity if it would help. She cares enough about him to know he needs a permanent home.' In seven cases at least one parent was opposed to permanent family placement of any sort.

These findings illustrate a change in child placement policy in two respects: first, a willingness to look for permanent substitute families, either with or without contact with natural parents, for children who have remained in residential care in part because their parents have continued to show some interest in them; and, secondly, a more towards the early placement of children in care, if necessary without the consent of their parents, and usually for adoption. Eight of the 12 children who had been in care for less than two years at referral were referred for adoption, and the other four were subsequently placed with parents who wished to adopt. In only four cases did both natural parents actually request adoption, and in one of these parental contact, and, in another, contact with grandparents and siblings, was requested. The parent of one child agreed reluctantly, and the parents of the other seven were opposed to adoption, though in six cases they agreed to 'permanent' fostering with contact.

THE CHILDREN AT THE TIME OF REFERRAL

At the time of referral the ages of the children ranged between seven months and 15 years. It can be seen from table 4.2 that the majority of the children were of school age but had not yet reached adolescence. From this it can be seen that, whilst all the children under five were placed, five of the seven children over 12 at referral were not placed. Put another way, 63 per cent of the children withdrawn were over 12 at the time of referral. Boys were slightly less likely to be placed than girls, but this difference is

Table 4.2 Age and sex at referral

Age in years	Boys			Girls				
	Placed	With-drawn	Total	Placed	With-drawn	Total	Total	%
Under 3	1	0	1	2	0	2	3	10
3–4	2	0	2	1	0	1	3	10
5–11	8	1	9	5	2	7	16	55
12+	1	4	5	1	1	2	7	24
Total	12	5	17	9	2	12	29	100

probably accounted for by the fact that a larger proportion of girls referred (83 per cent, as compared with 70 per cent of the boys) were under 12 at referral.

The main reasons for referral were given as Down's syndrome (two children), maladjustment (ten), being older (five), needing to be placed with siblings (eight), physical handicap (three) and legal problems (one child). However, from the detailed picture given in table 4.3 of each child referred, in terms of age, sex and the special needs identified at referral which might make placement difficult, it can be seen that for only one child was a single special need identified, and that for four children six 'obstacles to placement' were identified. Obstacles to placement were either individual difficulties of the child, such as physical or mental handicap, or being of an age when the likelihood of finding a new family was thought to be diminished; or related to the child's position in the family – for instance, the need to be placed with siblings or to remain in contact with parents or with siblings placed elsewhere, or the likelihood of a contested adoption. Sometimes one factor on its own would not have been a reason for referral to a specialist agency, but it became a contributory factor when combined with another source of potential difficulty, as with the five-year-old black child who had a mentally ill mother: the mother was likely to contest adoption and it was thought desirable for her to remain in contact with the child. One factor which did cause difficulties, but is not included in the table because it was never specifically mentioned by social workers, was institutionalization. To some extent it was one of the factors leading to inclusion in the

Table 4.3 The children in the case study: sex, age at referral, special needs identified at referral

Age	Sex M	Sex F	Down's syndrome	Physically handicapped	Mentally or educationally handicapped	Learning difficulties	Emotionally disturbed	Sibling group	Black/mixed race	Special school	Middle years	Adolescent	Natural family contact desirable	Legal complications likely	Total special needs
Children placed															
Babies (3)															
1		✓													1
1		✓	✓	✓											2
1	✓		✓	✓	✓										2
Toddlers (3)															
2	✓				✓			✓					✓	✓	3
4	✓					✓	✓	✓	✓				✓	✓	4
4		✓				✓		✓					✓	✓	3
Middle years (13)															
6	✓							✓			✓				2
7	✓			✓		✓	✓			✓	✓				4
7	✓			✓		✓	✓			✓	✓		✓		6
8		✓						✓			✓				2
8		✓						✓			✓				2
10	✓				✓	✓	✓	✓		✓	✓		✓		5
10	✓							✓	✓		✓		✓		3
10	✓					✓	✓	✓			✓		✓		6
11		✓						✓			✓		✓		3
11		✓			✓	✓	✓	✓			✓		✓		5
11	✓				✓	✓	✓	✓			✓		✓		6
11	✓							✓			✓		✓		6

Adolescents (2)														
12	✓					✓						✓	✓	4
14		✓				✓ ✓							✓	3
Sub-total	12	9	2	5	4	9	8	11	2	3	13	2	12	3
Children withdrawn														
Middle years (3)														
7	✓					✓	✓	✓			✓		✓	5
7	✓						✓	✓			✓		✓	3
10		✓				✓	✓				✓		✓	4
Adolescents (5)														
12	✓					✓				✓		✓		3
13		✓				✓	✓					✓		3
13	✓					✓	✓			✓		✓		4
14	✓					✓	✓			✓	✓	✓	✓	5
15	✓					✓	✓			✓	✓	✓	✓	5
Sub-total	5	3	0	2	0	6	6	2	2	3	16	5	6	1
Total	17	12	2	5	5	15	14	13	2	5	16	7	18	4

'emotional disturbance' category, but we considered that for ten children (seven boys and three girls) familiarity with and acceptance of an institutional way of life would be likely to create problems. This did not include all the children who were in residential care at the time of placement, and, indeed, we considered that ten children in residential care at the time of referral were not 'institutionalized'. Nine children were in foster care (six of those placed), and 20 were in residential care (15 of those placed).

Although children in residential care might have the extra problems associated with institutionalization, usually accompanied by difficulty in adjusting to family life, some of those in foster care had to negotiate the hurdle of leaving a foster family to which they had become attached and not really being able to understand why they had to move. We considered that this presented some difficulty to three of the older children who were placed. Some of those in residential care were also attached to those caring for them or enjoyed being where they were. We concluded from the evidence available, including interviews with the older children and psychological tests, that 15 were fairly happy in their present placements, while nine were fairly unhappy. 12 definitely wanted to move to a new family; 11 had mixed feelings; one definitely did not; and five were too young to be asked. Some of the children who were happy in their present placements welcomed the idea of a new permanent family, while those who were unhappy nevertheless had mixed feelings, usually associated with lack of self-esteem, fear of failure or anxiety about being disloyal to or losing contact with their birth parents.

On the evidence available we judged two children to have firm attachments to their caretakers at the time of referral, while eight were well on the way to becoming attached to one of the people caring for them. Although the others might have got on quite well with the people caring for them, we considered that they were not attached to any particular adult in a parenting role. This issue of 'bonding' or 'attachment' is central to any discussion of child placement. Many pages have been devoted to the question of whether it is better to have loved and lost than never to have loved at all. Since the publication of Bowlby's monograph (1951), perhaps the most helpful contributions to the debate are those of Erikson (1965, 1983) and Rutter (1972). We tried to assess from files and from discussions with social workers whether the children in our study had ever formed a trusting relationship with a natural or substitute parent – whether, in Winnicott's terms (1975) they had ever experienced for a long enough period of time the 'good-enough' parenting which allows for the establishment of personal identity and the growth of self-esteem. We judged that 15 of the children had formed at least one close and trusting attachment to a parent figure; that three, one aged two and two aged 11, had never had such a relationship, and that 11 had experienced one or more relationships with parent figure which were either partial or ambivalent. By *partial* we mean that the child was being given the sort of parental care which would encourage the development of attachment, but was moved before becoming fully attached. Typically this would apply to a baby who had received good care from temporary foster parents before being placed with a permanent family. However, some of the older children had had similar experiences, sometimes remaining in particular foster homes for years before some event, sometimes unconnected with the child, led to a move.

We noted that 19 of the children had been committed to care because of parental abuse (5) or neglect (14), and it was principally these children who were likely to have experienced *ambivalent* relationships with their parents, and subsequently with foster parents or residential workers. Lynch and Roberts (1982) have described the long-term effect which living with abusing parents can have on children. Because at times parents can be genuinely loving and offer good care, their children start to form loving relationships with them. However, they do not completely allow themselves to trust, as they learn from experience that, at times of depression or stress, this loving relationship will be withdrawn and they will be hurt physically or emotionally by the sometimes loving parent. Rutter (1972) stresses the importance of a child's temperament in determining whether or not it can surmount difficulties. Lynch and Roberts (1982) hypothesize that the abused children in their study who did well 'had successfully passed the developmental hurdle of basic trust (Erikson, 1965) and were therefore able to form good relationships'. It seemed to us on reading these children's case histories that some formed 'good-enough' attachments with more than one set of parents, whilst others went through their care careers as if surrounded by an invisible but impregnable wall which prevented anyone from coming near them.

The corollary of having become attached is that the child is more likely to be hurt by separation. Whilst the three children who had never become attached to a parent figure had never had to cope with the stress of separation from a loved and loving adult, 11 children experienced one separation from a parent figure to whom they were at least partially attached; 13 experienced two separations; and two became attached and separated from parent figures on three occasions. When discussing attachments in the context of children in care, it is important to note that often the only constant figure is a brother or sister, and that sometimes older siblings take on some of the practical and emotional roles of parents.

Before moving on to consider the children after referral, it seems important to describe them as people rather than mere statistics. Most of the parents said the descriptions they were given of the children before placement, including those given on their posters or in other publicity, were superficial and often inaccurate. Even the photo was often inaccurate, as, by the time they met him, the 11 year old whose photo they had fallen in love with might have turned into a gawky teenager with breaking voice and spots. Thus the new parents had gradually to piece together the child's history and present reality. As one adoptive mother put it, 'Talk about the past and painful areas comes out at funny times, like walking to catch a bus.'

In considering what sort of children these were, we found the most significant factors to be age, past experience and its impact on the child's personality and attitudes to placement.

The handicapped babies

The major problem in the placement of the three handicapped babies was the pressure of time. It is now widely accepted that progress made by handicapped infants, especially those with Down's syndrome, is greatly affected by the care they receive in their early months. Research studies, such as those by Gath (1983) and Macaskill (1985), are few, but suggest that in such cases the main problem for the agencies lies not in the behaviour of the child, but in the task of quickly finding a family with love, time and skill to give to a handicapped baby not born to them. The issues which are relevant to the placement of Down's babies are essentially those which are relevant to all baby adoptions. They differ in terms of the recruitment and preparation of the new families, rather than as regards the children themselves.

The main factors to be considered so far as the children are concerned are whether they have any additional emotional or physical difficulties and whether the transfer to the new home can be undertaken in such a way as to minimize any ill effects of separation. The two Down's children both came into care directly from hospital at the request of their parents. In both cases the parents were married, had other children and were greatly saddened by the experience of having a handicapped child whom they felt unable to care for. Both sets of parents requested adoptive placement and agreed to publicity, though in one case a placement with the possibility of contact was requested, and in the other grandparents put some pressure on the parents not to consent to adoption. One of the Down's babies was in excellent health but the other was described as a 'sickly, hypotonic baby who suffered from frequent projectile vomiting'. She was a tiny child whose attractiveness was not improved by the smell associated with vomiting. A new family would need to be able to spend time getting her to specialists, and to face the possibility that her frail health meant that any illness might be fatal.

The third child in this group was multiply handicapped, and the potential new family had to take on board considerable uncertainty about his future physical and mental abilities. He was cared for by his parents, with considerable help from grandparents and social services, until he was eight months old, but over the same period was twice admitted to hospital because of chest infections and failure to thrive. There was a gradual realization that there might be some degree of handicap, and tests following the second hospital admission and care proceedings indicated hearing loss, mild spasticity and possibly mental handicap. From hospital he went to a foster home, where he was given good care and seems to have become attached to his foster family. His parents visited weekly, and opposed placement either for adoption or long-term fostering, insisting that they wanted him home. Contact was terminated shortly before placement with a new family.

All three handicapped infants had been in foster care for several months. The child who was not taken into care until the age of eight months was 18 months at placement, and setting-in difficulties were reported. These probably were related to the loss of foster parents to whom he was at least partially attached. Both Down's babies were described by their new parents as settling in very quickly, apparently totally undisturbed by the move.

One of the Down's children was seen before placement by the researcher and psychologist, but it was not possible to see the other two children until after placement. Using the Griffiths Mental Development Scale, and observing play and personal social skills (Gunzberg, 1969), the three children were assessed as follows. A 13-month-old Down's child was retarded in her development by seven to eight months and was described as floppy and rather unattractive; an 18-month-old Down's child was retarded by eight months, but described as 'alert, active and cheerful'. Neither of these showed any sign of behaviour disturbance such as excessive screaming. The other child was seen at 22 months. His development showed a retardation of about a year. He was described as a cheerful, affectionate child, but his foster parents described some behaviour difficulties, especially his degree of activity and need for constant attention, and some head banging. His new family also described spasms of anger shortly after placement when he would attack a particular doll while not being aggressive with other toys. The adoptive father reported, 'For the first three or four weeks, it was something which really upset him. He used to bite it, shake it, get really angry. We don't know if he was taking his anger out on the doll, how he'd been treated. He could have been missing his foster parents.'

Apart from this, we were surprised how few reactions to separation from parent figures to whom they must have been well attached were reported by the new parents. It may be that the careful introductions minimized this, or it may be that the new families were not the most objective reporters of any signs of unhappiness, in that they were so happy to have the children with them at last that they could not allow for any unhappiness and therefore just failed to see it. Alternatively, they were so well prepared to expect problems that signs of distress appeared insignificant and, in their buoyant mood, they took them in their stride. It is important to look at positive aspects of the children as well as their problems. All three were described as loving and affectionate, and the time-consuming nature of the care needed was more than compensated for by their affectionate natures.

Pre-school children

To some extent the considerations for these three children were similar to those for babies, in the case of the youngest, or, for the two four-year-olds, to the older children in our study. Two were members of a sibling group, and two, by the time they were placed, were very definite personalities with firm recollections of their previous lives and affected by previous attachments. The youngest, who was nearly three at placement, was only 'hard to place' because he was a member of a sibling group. He was one of the three children whom we judged not to have formed any attachments with parent figures, but, given the acceptability of a two-year-old regressing to earlier stages of infancy and the willingness of his new parents to allow this (indeed, they welcomed it, as it helped their own attachment to develop quickly), this was not a problem. He was cared for by his mother until seven months old, but her depression led to poor care and it seems unlikely that he became attached to her before being placed in care. The next eight months he spent in two different children's homes. He then spent four months at home 'on trial' with his mother, but care again deteriorated and he spent the next 13 months in the same children's home as before. Throughout this time he was constantly with one of his siblings and in close contact with the others, with whom he was eventually placed. His difficult behaviour on placement had more to do with institutionalization than with separation, since his only constant companions, his siblings, moved with him. He had already learned, for example, that, if one adult says 'No', there may be another who will say 'Yes.' His adoptive father reported, 'He had temper tantrums. He couldn't understand that when Jenny said no, there was no one else to go to.'

To some extent his adaptation to family life was made more difficult, as well as being helped, by being with his siblings. He was sensitive to their difficulties, whilst not understanding them, and was influenced by the mood swings of the brothers and sisters he cared about. Although separation from his natural mother was of no significance to him, as he had hardly known her, he was a party to their conversations about her, and the pace and manner of discussion about adoption was dictated more by their needs than by his. This also applied to his sister, who was five when placed and had a similar background, except that she was ambivalently attached to her mother and knew and cared about her as a real person. Because of the different time scales involved, these two children moved in before their older siblings. Another problem associated with life in residential care and placement with a sibling was jealousy. The inability to rely on loving and trusted adults who will meet one's needs inevitably leads to competition for whatever love and affection is to be had, and jealousy was a feature of the behaviour of both children when they moved in with their new families.

Although referred at four, both older children in this group were of school age when they were placed. Both sets of parents said independently that they greatly regretted that they had sent the children to school immediately after placement. One couple did so against their better judgement and under some pressure from social workers, and eventually withdrew the child from school. The other family only later came to realize that going to school had made it more difficult for their daughter to go through the stage of regression which is necessary and still acceptable with children of this age. The special problems of these children were in having to function at two levels – that appropriate to their real age, and that appropriate to the stage of their relationship with their new parents. They were also both of average or above average intelligence and were anxious to weigh up what was the right way to behave. Both had experienced separations from people to whom they were at least partially attached, and both had lived with parents who loved them and showed them affection at times but also behaved unpredictably. Their behaviour was therefore controlled and wary, and tension would suddenly break out in the form of violent outbursts in the case of one, nightmares and withdrawn behaviour in the case of the other. The anxiety engendered by trying to do the right thing was increased by the enormous changes for both of them in their way of life. Both moved from urban to rural environments, from the cut and thrust of, in one case, a large foster home and urban street life, and, in the other, a children's home, to the smaller scale and different expectations of middle or upper-class family life. One particular source of frustration was their inability to amuse themselves, having been used to constant distractions.

Two of these children showed fairly severe behaviour problems; one, almost none at all. His sunny disposition quickly made its mark on his new family: 'We couldn't have hoped for anyone better. He is a lovely, lovely child.' For the two older children a Rutter parent scale was completed by the previous caretakers, and all three were seen by the research psychologist. All three were of average or above average intelligence but showed signs of immaturity. None was scored as being disturbed on the parent Rutter scale. Two of the children showed no signs of emotional disturbance when interviewed by the psychologist, although their new parents did report some disturbed behaviour. The third showed signs of unhappiness and aggressive feelings. However, these quotations from two of the psychologists's reports are of interest:

The main themes in play were associated with mother figures, and ghosts. The boy on the horse beat up the ghosts and the mummy.

She seems to see the world as an unhappy place where she feels powerless.

His play was disorganized in approach and I felt he lacked internal controls. He has aggressive feelings towards his mother figures which may cause him some problems in his new home. He is an emotionally deprived child who, despite his chirpy, bumptious façade, is unhappy.

Clearly, with children of this age a longer introduction is needed, and it should be remembered that the children themselves are old enough to have views and might not like the families chosen for them. All three children were well prepared by their caretakers before they met their new parents, and the two eldest were saying that they wanted to move to a permanent family. One was confused, however, by the fact that a younger sibling was still being cared for by the natural mother, and wondering what there was about her which made this not possible in her case.

The older children

We consider the 15 school-age children together, as the seven and eight-year-olds had much in common with the 13-year-olds, and distinctions has less to do with the children's age then with the reasons for their being 'hard to place'. Several writers have commented on the problems of placing teenagers with foster or adoptive families (Fallon et al., 1983; Hipgrave, 1983). Our study has led us to conclude that age alone is not a good guide to whether placement of a teenager is likely to be successful or not, and that more significant indicators are, on the one hand, motivation to be part of a new family, and, on the other, attachment to previous caretakers, interest in forming relationships with members of the opposite sex and interest in moving towards independence. Thus one fourteen-year-old was placed after nearly two years of trying because she urged her social worker not to give up looking for a new family for her. Another fourteen-year-old, who had no links with his natural family, hated the children's home he was in and had suffered several failed attempts at permanence, overcame his fear of yet another rejection and was successfully placed. Another teenager in residential care very much liked the new family she was introduced to after two years of waiting. But in the interim she had settled in the home she had lived in for many years, and she chose to stay near her boyfriend and move towards independence from a base where she felt comfortable.

Two children had had apparently normal and reasonably happy lives until their mothers died and the attempts of other family members to care for them collapsed. Their feelings about finding a new family obviously were different from those of children who had few warm and happy memories of natural parents. Principally, they were more likely to be beset by anxieties about disloyalty to their natural families if they allowed themselves to be adopted, and were anxious to keep in touch with family members about whom they had good feelings. The only child who initially was definitely opposed to the idea of being placed with a new family was one of these two. The other went along with the idea at an intellectual level because he was unhappy in his present placement. However, his sense of loyalty would not allow him to give himself to the new parents when he was introduced to them. The first child, having strongly resisted the idea of moving from his foster home, which was close to his extended family, was lucky enough to find a new family resilient and skilled enough to provide him with the security of a permanent home whilst facilitating continued contact with members of his natural family. He was also fortunate in that his attractive personality and loving nature – how much due to temperament, how much a tribute to the earlier 'good-enough' care? – which shone through all the sadness of the loss of his mother, the unsuccessful attempt to live with his father and step-mother, and the loss of close contact with siblings and grand-parents, gave his new family a ready incentive. That he was also physically handicapped is an extra complication which almost seems incidental compared with these problems associated with attachment and loss.

Thanks often to the painstaking, courageous and insistent 'life story' work of previous caretakers, new parents, some natural parents, local authority and project social workers, we found that several of the children had clear pictures of their lives before coming into care. Others, especially the younger ones, might have a fairly simplistic picture, but it was one which they had grown to accept and live with. Peter, aged nine, explained, 'My mum and dad had difficulty paying the rates bill, so they decided to get rid of me.'

For several children the most difficult thing to understand and accept was why *they* were not being cared for by their parents when other siblings were. Given a tendency to low self-esteem, they all too readily assumed, and sometimes told us, that it was because there was something wrong with them. This was, in fact, close to the truth for two children, whose physical handicaps did make them more difficult to care for, and it would hardly have been surprising if this had made them even more angry about their handicaps. The children who had been abused seemed, in their interviews with us, to take this in their stride. One lad who had been abused when he was old enough to remember was convinced that all his problems dated from when the interfering social worker had taken him to hospital. Otherwise he would still be at home. He had since lost touch with his parents and was very anxious to be adopted.

Some of the children had to make sense of the loss not only of their natural parents, but also of other families they had grown to love. We noted above that some children had allowed themselves to become attached twice more after losing their first parents. Others had put their defences up after being hurt once. Those who had had more than one placement seemed able to differentiate between placements which were not meant to be permanent and those which were. Two children who had had unsuccessful adoptive placements refused to talk to us about them, but spoke with warmth and no bitterness about foster homes where they had been happy. One eight-year-old had at least three pairs of 'other mums and dads' in his background whom he chatted on about. In talking about his sadness at leaving one such much and dad, and wondering if they remembered him, he said in a matter of fact way, 'People forget you are around, and they think about the people who *are* around.'

Some of the previous mums and dads, whether natural or foster parents, had tried to help the children to move on emotionally. It was, however, a difficult time when an older child moved from foster parents where there was mutual affection, and the introductory period was especially stressful if, as on two occasions, the foster parents would have liked the child to stay with them as a foster child and were not fully convinced of the need for a move to an adoptive home. We were unfortunately not able to interview either set of foster parents, but were told by the social workers that they tried to hide their feelings in the interest of the child.

Those children who were still in touch with their parents seemed to suffer whether or not their parents consented to adoption. If the parents signed consent forms and especially if there were other children at home, they asked themselves what was so wrong with them that they could be so easily 'signed away'. One teenager, when the social worker said that her father had signed consent to adoption, was angry at his 'signing her away, just like that'. An eight-year-old cried when told that her mother had signed the consent and asked to see her mother again. Some natural parents tried to help their children by writing to tell them why they thought they should be adopted; others said that 'they' (the social workers) thought it was best, partly to shift the blame from themselves, partly because they thought it would not be helpful to the children to think that their parents had not wanted them. For this reason, some agreed verbally to permanent placement without contact but refused to sign consent to adoption. Others said they might agree to adoption once they knew that the children were happily settled. If a parent had died fairly recently, there was the added complication of 'death-bed promises' to stay together as a family and the child's sense, whether conscious or not, that to give itself to a new mother and father, would be an act of disloyalty to the dead parent.

There were particular problems for two older members of sibling groups who, though attracted by the idea of a new family, were attached to their natural parents and might, if they had not also been attached to their siblings, have been able to return home. The social workers made the final decision for them, but they could not protect the children from awareness that there was a choice to be made. One older brother of two boys placed later and not included in the main study did decide at the last moment that he could not make the move to new parents.

It is hardly surprising that these awesome decisions had an impact on the children, both at the time and later. Work with the children on their backgrounds was a continuing process as they strove to find their identities, and it was very common for a child's sense of hurt to return at such times. Some coped by hurting the people nearest to them in physical or verbal outbursts of aggression. One little boy reacted by withdrawing emotionally from the adoptive parents who were trying so hard to make him part of their family and telling them that he wanted to tell his social worker that they were not looking after him properly. This same child had told a previous potential adoptive mother that his favourite mother was 'the pretty one with the white hair' (his natural mother).

Others coped by rationalizations, looking for practical reasons (such as the illness of a foster mother) why they had had to leave previous homes, and if they could find a convincing practical reason it seemed to make it safer to talk about the good things in the home. One group of children whose previous attempt at permanence had failed when the foster mother had fallen ill needed a great deal of reassurance about the physical health of the adoptive parents to whom they were being introduced.

Most of the children showed symptoms of separation from parent figures to whom they had felt some affection. At least two of the older children had not had the opportunity to become close to parents or substitute parents, and they both showed the symptoms classically associated with maternal deprivation (Bowlby, 1951, 1977; Rutter, 1972). Adults were not to be trusted and were to be outwitted in the pursuit of whatever the children had set their minds on at the time. Having decided that he wanted a new family, one youngster was able to behave so perfectly when he met his potential new family that the foster parents felt he had been 'coached' on how to behave. As soon as he was placed, he began, his foster mother reported, a pattern of 'thieving and lying which I found it almost impossible to take'. Other children showed less obvious symptoms of a lack of basic trust and these were often combined with behaviour usually associated with spending long periods in residential care. One mother commented of her foster son 'We don't know if he has a conscience. Things are only wrong because they get you sent away.' Like the younger children, such children attempted to play one member of the new family off against another and, as several of the new parents put it, 'had difficulty taking no for an answer'.

On the other hand, in terms of what can loosely be described as 'manners', the expectations of children's homes or boarding schools and those of the new parents broadly agreed. Only two children, who moved from working-class foster homes into professional families, found themselves in a world whose mores were very different from what they were used to.

Brothers and sisters

Members of sibling groups who got on well with each other and had similar attitudes to change had the advantage, in coping with the strangeness of the introductory and settling-in period, of being able to share their feelings. With brothers and sisters, the need to place them together usually took precedence over their individual, often different needs, particularly the need to remain in contact with their natural parents or other relatives which was sometimes considered desirable for (and by) older children, but was generally considered undesirable for younger children. Thus members of the same family were, during the introductory period, watching each other for signs of disloyalty to the natural parents, as when one older girl who had 'mothered' her younger brothers and sisters and had hoped to return to her natural mother told her younger brother off for calling his new parents 'mum and dad'. A youngster in such a position will also have mixed emotions about letting go of the responsibility and power of 'parenthood' and will not immediately welcome the chance to catch up on her own childhood and the mothering she has missed. Jealousy, squabbling and competition for the affections of new parents were also common between siblings, as was anxiety either that one of their brothers or sisters would not want to move or that the new family would not want one of them. Speaking of the introductory period one new mother said, 'The complexity with these children is that they are all worrying about what each other is doing and saying, and if they are doing it right. Every time they had to go back there were crying matches.'

With all these extra difficulties one might conclude that it would be better to meet the needs of each child individually, if necessary by placing them separately. This happened with three older physically handicapped children, two of whom remained in care when other siblings returned home, and one of whom was placed quite a long way from older brothers and sisters to whom he was attached, thus adding to the difficulties of the new parents in keeping up the contact which they had promised him and believed to be desirable. In the opinion of this mother,

These four children really should not have been separated. He is attached to them, but there is the love–hate thing. They bully him. We don't bawl and swear at him and poke him as they do. I would have liked contact to be very regular, have them down here to stay, but it didn't work out to be so easy. They don't want what is best for him. They want what is best for their conscience. They are guilty because they promised they would all stay together.

As this comment indicates, if siblings placed elsewhere were in agreement with the placement, as was sometimes the case, continued contact by letter, phone calls or visits could ease the separation and be comfortable for all concerned. If the separate placement was opposed, contact caused discomfort.

In two cases social workers deliberately looked for a childless couple or a family with older children because they felt that children of the natural family would be pushed out by a cohesive group. In one case where two siblings from a much larger family were placed together, they could not work out why this was done. Each was jealous when the other had a better relationship with the children in the new family; they were unable to agree what story to tell their new friends about their background; and they seemed embarrassed by each other's presence. David, aged thirteen, said, 'They put us together because they thought we got on really well together. But we don't!'

Children with physical disabilities

Three of these children were of school age, and a one-year-old was deaf and almost certainly mentally handicapped as well. For the older children their disability presented some extra problems, but, as Wolkind and Kozaruk (1986) also found in their study of children with medical difficulties placed for adoption through the ARE, these were minor compared with the problems of separation and being in care which they shared with the other school-age children. They tended to be lower in self-esteem because of their handicap, especially if they saw this as the reason why their natural family did not want them. In one case this showed itself in the form of intense competitiveness. If they had to attend special school, this could necessitate travelling long distances and leave little time for play on returning home, compounding the problem, for children who couldn't just go out and run around with the rest, of not being able to make friends easily. On the other hand, this reduced mobility meant that, if the child was prepared to accept the frustration of not going out to play, the increased time spent at home with mum and dad allowed for the attachment process to happen more quickly. Also, the fact that more physical care was needed made regression more acceptable. There were indications that the desperate need of handicapped children to be 'ordinary' made them want to fit in with their new families quickly. All three of the older children with physical handicaps quickly took on the surname of their new parents, used 'mum and dad' to refer to them to others, and were anxious to be adopted.

Black or mixed race children

We have already noted that, for the one black and one mixed race child in the study, race was not the factor which made either 'hard to place'. In one case the child had been living with a black foster mother and placement with a black family was considered desirable. However, no black family was found who would accept the legal complexities, and he was therefore placed with white parents who had a good understanding of the culture from which he came and who had black friends. This child appeared quickly to take on a white identity, saying that he liked his white family and appearing embarrassed when he visited Brixton with his new parents. The mixed race child had white siblings and a previous long-term placement with a white family had ended when the foster father died. The need for continued contact with siblings was considered to take precedence over any possible need to place him with a black family who might be more able to help him with his identity. No social worker we interviewed mentioned that placement with a black or mixed race family had been considered. At the time of placement he preferred to see himself as white, and at the two-year stage he was so firmly attached to his new family that he persuaded himself that he had been born to his new parents:

> *Peter*　I couldn't ever call anyone dad who isn't my real dad.
> *Dad*　　But you do – me.
> *Peter*　Well, I suppose I do.

Both sets of new parents were conscious of the need to find ways of helping the children to find a comfortable identity as black or mixed race children in a white society (Gill and Jackson, 1982). Two years after placement was too early to judge whether they had succeeded, especially for the younger child, but the older one, then aged 14, was one of those who had made very good progress and whose well-being we rated as high. His parents commented,

Ways of helping him. We practise at home. We talk about his colour – joke about it – well that's what other people will do. But always in a loving way. If you ignored his colour, he may think there is something wrong. If you spoke seriously about it, he'd think it funny. You have to joke with him.

PSYCHOLOGICAL ASSESSMENTS OF CHILDREN AT REFERRAL

In assessing the older children prior to or at the time of placement, the psychologist looked at their self-esteem, their intellectual potential and achievement, and any signs of emotional or behavioural disturbance. The Rutter scales (Rutter, 1975) which had been completed by previous caretakers of the children placed and of those withdrawn also gave indications of emotional or behavioural disturbance.

Although educational handicap was not given as the major reason for referral to a specialist agency for any of the children, learning difficulties were a problem in 16 cases. Several children of average ability were under-achieving, and this applied to all three physically handicapped children, where there were discrepancies between performance scores and verbal scores. The performance scores were lower, but this was to be expected because of the clumsiness produced by the handicap. With the other children, any discrepancy tended to be in the other direction, with higher performance than verbal scores. This was especially the case for children from disturbed backgrounds. Of the 19 children old enough to be assessed, two were considered to be of above average intelligence; 13 were average; two were assessed as moderately educationally handicapped (ESN(M)), and two as severely educationally handicapped (ESN(S)).

We noted a difference between boys and girls in the degree of identified behavioural and emotional disturbance at referral. Rutter scales were available for 16 of the children placed and for five of those withdrawn. They indicated no disturbance for eight of the children placed and for one withdrawn. The scales indicated that eight of the children placed and four of those withdrawn had some disturbance, six showing signs of neurotic behaviour and six of anti-social behaviour. This is a higher rate of disturbance than found by other researchers using the same scale with children in care – 57 per cent, as compared with 46 per cent for Wolkind's sample of children in residential care (Wolkind, 1974) and 37 per cent for Thorpe's sample of children in foster care (Thorpe, 1974). Using these scales, psychologist's reports and, for children not seen by the research psychologist, psychological assessments on file, we rated all the children for behvaiour and emotional disturbance at the time of referral.

More than half the boys and only one of the girls had moderate or marked disturbance of behaviour at referral, as shown by destructiveness, stealing, temper tantrums and other forms of aggressive behaviour. Amongst the symptoms indicating emotional disturbance were nervous tics, picking at clothing or parts of the body, extreme anxiety about anything new, and obsessional behaviour.

20 children were assessed as showing signs of emotional disturbance, and for ten of these (eight boys and two girls) this was either moderate or marked. Of the 15 older children seen by the psychologist at referral, six were assessed as having positive self-esteem and two fairly positive. Two were assessed as high in some respects, low in others, and six were considered to have low self-esteem. Emotional adjustment and well-being were assessed for the younger children by use of the Lowenfeld Word Technique (Lowenfeld, 1979), by direct observation of the children and by talking with the parents about their behaviour.

Putting these various measures together, we concluded that the well-being of five of the children was average; that for 14 (48 per cent) there was some reason for concern; and that ten (35 per cent) had problems which were considered serious (six) or severe (four). All those in this latter category were boys.

Whilst only 28 per cent of those placed had serious or severe problems, this was the case with 50 per cent of those withdrawn. This figure is influenced by the fact that more older children were withdrawn, and older children were more likely to have problems.

We conclude from this information that the CWAH was indeed attempting to find homes for children many of whom would be likely to experience difficulties after placement.

SUMMARY

The children referred came roughly equally from two groups. Those who had been in care for several years had mostly lived in reisdential care, often with siblings and usually still in contact with parents or siblings placed elsewhere. These children were typical of the 'children who wait' identified by Rowe and Lambert (1973), except that they were more likely than those in Rowe's sample to be in contact with members of the natural family. Towards the end of the project an increasing proportion of those referred came from a second category comprising children of all ages who had been in care for comparatively short periods, and who were consequently still likely to be in touch with natural parents. Some of their parents were opposed to permanent placement, whilst others were pleased that family placement was available to children whom they were unable or unwilling to care for themselves.

All were in the categories of 'special need' identified by the project, and most had more than one characteristic which was likely to cause difficulties in finding a suitable placement. The children referred included some who were physically or mentally handicapped and older children with behavioural or educational problems. Almost half had been abused or neglected. 23 (79 per cent) were over five at referral, and 13 (45 per cent) were over 12 by the time they were either placed or withdrawn. At the time of referral, 18 (62 per cent) wanted to stay in contact with a member of their natural family.

Previous attempts at permanent placement had been made for 13 (45 per cent) of the children, sometimes on more than one occasion. Most were still in need of family placement not because of lack of planning, but because previous plans had not worked out, or because they had come into care at a time when it was considered more important for them to be placed with siblings and stay in touch with parents, aims that could more readily be achieved by the use of residential care.

5

The Children after Placement

When they aren't talking they are shouting. When they aren't shouting they are arguing. When they are asleep they are talking in their sleep or falling out of bed. They drain everything out of you. You don't know if you are thinking straight.

(Foster mother of teenage brothers)

THE WAITING TIME

We were able to monitor 14 children during the period when they were waiting for new families. These were the children referred directly; those referred indirectly only came to our attention once a project family had been identified as sufficiently likely to provide a suitable home for introductions to start. Only three of the 14 waited for less than nine months before placement, four were placed between 12 and 18 months after referral, and two between 18 months and two years. Two were withdrawn after nine months, two after 12 months and one after 18 months. This is important as some social workers and managers seriously underestimate the time needed to place children in permanent homes. This may have unfortunate consequences if unrealistic time limits are placed on the 'bridge' or assessment placements, which are increasingly being used in order to determine whether permanence should be achieved through planned return home or through substitute family placement (Wilcox, 1983). If, as is sometimes the case, time limits of six, or even three, months are set on transition placements, it is almost inevitable that an unnecessary move will be involved. This happened for only one of the children in the study, but the threat of home closure led to pressure to place some children more quickly than was thought desirable.

All the children who were referred directly and not placed were over ten. One youngster had waited too long, and, although she liked the family she was introduced to, and they her, she was more interested in setting up a home of her own than in becoming a daughter to new parents. Although the others had apparently wanted to join permanent new families, all still had strong feelings about natural parents. One teenager told the psychologist that he wanted to be adopted until he was old enough to go to live with his dad. Three of the children who were introduced to new families were surprised and hurt when the introduction proved unsuccessful. In two cases the family did not measure up in important respects to the needs of the children as expressed at the planning meetings. This may have weakened their confidence in the possibility of a new home being found. Although there were other families interested in meeting them, two of these children preferred to 'lick their wounds' in familiar territory and renewed their hopes of returning home. At the end of the study period two (not the same two) were placed with natural fathers, and the social workers expressed satisfaction with the placements and felt that the children's well-being had improved since the time of referral. In another case the placement matched the child's needs ideally, and child and new family expressed a liking for each other. However, this boy was particularly disturbed, and the enormity of the step he had agreed to take, emphasized by the distance he had to travel for each visit, seemed to impose too much stress. A spectauclar piece of delinquent behaviour convinced the project worker and the family that the placement could not recover from such a bad start. It was decided that at 15 he had missed the boat and that his behaviour indicated that he did not really want a family placement. It was our view, in the light of a lengthy interview and the psychologist's assessment, that he did want to live with a family but was overwhelmed, at least at that stage, by the discomfort of having to lose one mum and dad and accept another. We were inclined to agree with his local authority worker that a 'treatment' or 'professional' foster placement would have been more appropriate. One boy had not been introduced to a new family after 18 months. The research psychologist who interviewed him at this stage described him as appearing unrealistically high in self-esteem: 'Jim did not seem anxious and he seemed remarkably unconcerned about the delay in finding him a foster home.' At a subsequent interview with his project worker he seemed so unconcerned as to give the impression that he was not interested in finding a new home and he was withdrawn from the project. However, his residential worker felt that he had been genuinely interested but had given up hope as time wore on and was, at the end, 'whistling in the dark' to keep his spirits up.

A delay in placement is particularly significant for older children, who can quickly change from children to young adults. This happened with several children in our study. The ages on their posters were changed, but the photos of them and specifications of the sort of home they required became seriously outdated. This extract from a research interview with one of the three teenagers withdrawn from the project found echoes in interview with the others.

Researcher	Who would you say loves you most?
Alec	Don't know. (*Pause*) My old mum.
Researcher	Who do you love most?
Alec	(*Without any hesitation*) My old mum.
Researcher	Can you remember how you felt when your social worker talked to you about finding a new family?
Alec	A load of old rubbish. Just rubbish. Nothing interesting.
Researcher	What do you think your mum thought about it?
Alec	She would have had to agree to it. It would depend how far. If it was near, it would be easier for me to get to mum.

He expressed himself in the same way at the final interview, after new initiatives for finding a home had been put to him:

Alec	It was a dead bore. I kind of slept through it. I was tired of waiting.
Researcher	If it was quicker, would you have gone?
Alec	Probably. If I had a choice, I would have gone to mum. But, if there was no choice, I would probably have given it a try.

From talking to the residential worker and social worker, we concluded that at the referral stage he had been genuinely interested in living in a new home, though secretly promising himself that whatever the social workers said he would keep in touch with his natural mother. As time went on, in order to cope with the blow to his self-esteem of being advertised but not wanted, he retreated into bravado and convinced himself that nothing significant had happened. To those seeing him occasionally he put on a 'joky' front and appeared not to care whether a placement was found. However, his residential worker said the waiting was 'tearing him apart'.

A long wait, or even an abortive introduction, need not mean that a child will not be placed. Three teenagers were placed after more than 12 months had elapsed before they were even introduced to a family. The delay for three other children from the same family was the consequence of making sure that return to the natural family really did have to be ruled out. Only two of the seven children withdrawn (siblings aged under ten) had been placed with a permanent foster family two years after withdrawal. It would seem, at least from this small number, that a long wait or an introduction which fails is likely to stand in the way of placement, especially for older children, and especially if there are emotional links, however unsatisfactory or unrealistic, with natural parents.

THE FIRST TWO YEARS AFTER PLACEMENT

In chapter 7 we shall consider the children as members of their new families, but we include here some descriptive material about their behaviour after placement. We also consider in chapter 7 the nature and pace of their growing attachment to their new families, and it is in the context of the stresses inevitably imposed by this major task of finding a place for themselves in the emotional and practical lives of existing family members that we must view the children's behaviour. The extensive descriptive and research literature on foster care and adoption referred to in chapter 1 speaks of a 'honeymoon period' followed by a period of 'testing out'. This spell of more difficult and often apparently irrational or self-destructive behaviour is sometimes interpreted as asking, 'Can I really trust them to love me when they know how unlovable I really am?'; sometimes, especially with more disturbed children, as signifying, 'I will force them to reject me to prove to myself that I am in control of the situation and cannot be let down as I was in the past'; and sometimes as likely to facilitate attachment to the new parent figure (see especially Fahlberg, 1981, and Jewett, 1978, 1984). We found support for the thesis that behaviour which appears disturbed, abnormal or immature may serve a useful function in helping new parents and children to become attached to one another, but also that it carried risks in terms of the strain imposed on other relationships in the family. Regression to babyhood and 'acting out' behaviour such as temper tantrums were often described, and may have had the same effect as a baby's cry in bringing comfort from the closeness with a parent. As one mother said, 'In a funny way, the problems made him get closer.'

We used two check lists to get a picture of the children in their new homes at various stages, and of any difficult behaviour. Most of the children were fairly well behaved in the early weeks, and the parents frequently commented that they wondered why social workers had painted such a bleak picture. 'We had a report on their personalities. Peter was blown up out of all proportion', one mother said, while another commented, 'Jim was supposed to have a violent temper. We haven't seen any of that.' Only three children, all teenagers who were placed from residential care, showed difficult behaviour right from the start. More often the 'honeymoon' period carried on through the introduction and for several weeks into the placement, though in the majority of cases the fact that 'normal' behaviour for the child was different from 'normal' behaviour in the family was something of a strain. This particularly applied to such things as shouting, running noisily up and down stairs, and needing to be entertained – some children seemed unable to amuse themselves even for short periods of time. Noisiness was the feature of their behaviour which most readily came to mind (mentioned 14 times). Other descriptions used at this stage were 'immature', 'sulky', 'secretive', 'quarrelsome', 'suspicious', 'moody', 'erratic' and 'clinging'. During this early period the children were very much wanting to belong, and we were told on more than one occasion of older children asking the parents or siblings to help them behave appropriately.

The 'honeymoon' period lasted for varying lengths of time, perhaps the shortest being three weeks in the case of the child who was removed. Four or five months was more normal. One father reported, 'We had a long good period, and then after about five or six months the things they said about them started to come true.' Sometimes there was no obvious 'testing out' period. The children became more relaxed and allowed themselves to be 'normally' naughty, and the parents allowed themselves to become cross and have their off days too. Sometimes, especially if they had had several placements, children would still be trying desperately hard to please even at the two-year stage, as with the youngster we interviewed whose major worry each morning was 'what mood mum will be in'. (It should be said that 'mum' was not at all a moody person.) However, this desperate attempt to be good so as not to be sent away imposed too much stress, which was likely to show itself in outbursts of particularly difficult behaviour or uncharacteristic episodes of delinquency. Descriptions often used of children in this later stage were 'excessively noisy', 'deceitful', 'lying', 'hyperactive', 'destructive', 'excessively quarrelsome', 'grizzling', 'aggressive' and 'sexually provocative'. Temper tantrums, stealing and bed-wetting occurred in some cases. It should be said that parents did not always see them as indications of problems, although they imposed stress on the households, as when grizzling and shouting were seen as normal behaviour for a Down's toddler. The average number of problems mentioned per child was between three and four; the lowest was none and the highest eight.

Besides asking the ten children we interviewed about their past lives and how they were getting on in their new homes, we asked what sort of person they were, again using a check list. All except two ticked more positive statements than negative, but two whom we considered not to be well attached had a very negative view of themselves. One youngster, who was very anxious not to be sent away, ticked and 'never' box for 'nice to know' and 'loving', and the 'mostly' box for 'sulky', 'noisy', 'bad-tempered' and 'naughty'. When asked why he thought his parents had chosen him, he said rather sadly, 'Hm. That's what I'd like to know.'

THE CHILDREN 18 MONTHS TO TWO YEARS AFTER
PLACEMENT OR WITHDRAWAL

We were able to obtain psychological assessments on all but four of the children placed, and for three of these we had the Rutter parent and teacher scales, as well as the descriptions given by their new parents and the project workers. For the remaining youngster we had to rely on the social worker for an assessment of progress and well-being. We were only able to interview three youngsters after they had been withdrawn from the project. However, the social workers of all the children who had been withdrawn answered a telephone questionnaire at the two-year stage about the current placement and any other changes, the child's reactions to withdrawal from the project, and the social workers' own views about whether the child's well-being had improved or deteriorated since referral to the project.

At the two-year stage 25 of the 29 children were living as members of their own or a substitute family. Two of the others were growing fairly successfully towards independence, and only two were, according to their social workers, in placements where their current needs were not being met, making it necessary to seek new placements. Nine CWAH-placed children had been adopted, and 12 were in 'secure' foster homes – seven with, and five without, contact with members of their birth families living elsewhere. Two of the children withdrawn were in 'secure' foster homes with no contact with their natural family and were likely to be adopted, and two were living with natural parents. Two were in the same residential unit, and two had moved to bedsitter accommodation. The exact type of placement originally planned for was achieved for only 11 of the 29 children (eight where plans were for adoption without contact, and three where fostering with contact was achieved). Five of the adoption hearings took place in the first 12 months, and two more within 18 months.

Actual contact with either parents or siblings living elsewhere continued after placement in seven of the 11 cases where either of the social workers thought it desirable. However, only seven of the 14 children who would have liked to continue to see either parents or siblings living elsewhere did so after placement. For 15 children, at least one parent either wanted the child home or wanted continued contact, but in only three cases did contact continue. No adopted child was in contact with either a parent or a sibling living elsewhere, although there was a possibility of this happening for one adopted child, and for two children who were likely to be adopted and remained in contact with siblings or relatives. 11 of the children, all those for whom it was thought desirable, were placed with brothers or sisters.

In our introductory remarks we noted the difficulty of talking about permanence in a society where the nuclear and extended family are less permanent than they used to be. We asked social workers and new parents to assess whether the children would still be with them in five years time or, for teenagers, whether they would still, at the end of that period, be regular visitors to the family home, even though they might have set up homes of their own. We considered that 14 (67 per cent) had found, to use Triseliotis's term, 'a family for life, with its network of support systems, not only for them, but also for their future children'

(1983, p. 24). We thought this might be the case for another four, but probably not for the remaining three, although all were likely to stay in the placement till they reached 18 or moved to independent living. Two children, we have since learned, moved out at 17, but one is in fairly close touch with her foster mother though not with other members of the family. Some of the children were too old at placement, or too damaged by what had gone before, or too ambivalent about exchanging one set of parents for another, to be able to adapt to the real give and take of close family life. However, they may have learned something from their new families about the satisfactions and demands of close relationships, and this may help them in the relationships they form as adults. In the light of the evidence available, we assessed that 19 of the children (14 placed, five withdrawn) were well or fairly well attached to at least one parent figure at the two-year stage.

Although our main aim was to describe what happened to the children, we were interested in trying to tease out why some children fared better than others. The numbers involved counsel caution, as they are too small for tests of statistical significance. Using the two measures of success which most closely reflect the purpose of the agency – to find permanent placements, and, in so doing, to enable the children to develop attachments to parents which would assist them in overcoming their handicaps, including that of being in long-term care – we looked for descriptive purposes, at a number of variables in the children and new families which might be linked with these measures. In so doing we included for most of the variables all 29 children referred, as we were satisfied that on questions of attachment and permanence the social workers' assessments of the eight children withdrawn were reliable. We concluded that a child who was well or fairly well attached to at least one parent figure at the two-year stage was more likely than those who were not

- to be female;
- to have been under 12 at placement (all those under five at placement were well attached; all the under-12s were at least fairly well attached; 69 per cent of the over-12s were not considered to be even fairly well attached);
- to have been in care for less than six years at placement (all but one in this category), though it is encouraging to note that a third of those in care for six years or more had also formed reasonable attachments;

- to have been in foster care as the main placement (though caution is needed here, as most of those whose main placement was a foster home were younger and therefore more likely to be well attached on that account);
- to have experienced more than one care episode (an interesting point – perhaps the children with only one care episode had not satisfied themselves that living with natural parents was no longer possible for them; this could usefully be tested with larger numbers and is in agreement with the conclusion of the much larger American study reported by Fein et al., 1983);
- to have had fewer than four placements in the last care episode (but there was hardly any difference between those with only one placement and those with two or three);
- to have had a 'good-enough' attachment to a previous parent figure (14 of the 15 children who had formed a previous attachment, as against only six of the 14 who were thought not to have done – a finding that supports the view that children who have had a good experience of parenting can more easily withstand the pain of separation and become attached to new parents: 11, or 69 per cent, of the 16 children who had experienced two or more separations from parent figures to whom they had had some attachment were at least fairly well attached to new parents at the two-year stage);
- to be a child for whom the main 'handicap' to placement was legal problems, or the fact of being a Down's baby, physically handicapped, an older child or a member of a sibling group (on the other hand, 67 per cent of those whose main obstacle to placement was said to be maladjustment or institutionalization were not even fairly well attached);
- to have come into care for reasons other than abuse or neglect (53 per cent of those who had been abused or neglected were at least fairly well attached, as compared with 100 per cent of those who had not been);
- to be rated as of average or above average well-being at placement;
- to have definitely wanted to find a permanent new family.

On the whole this list simply confirms what one might have expected, but it does serve to warn against hoping for too much too quickly from children with a different profile. Other characteristics were less clear cut. There was no relationship between whether a child was in contact with natural parents at placement and subsequent attachment to new parents, though a child who wanted continued contact was less likely to be attached, irrespective of whether the contact was continued or terminated. The two children who have recently left their new homes had no contact with natural parents, and the child whose first CWAH placement was disrupted had none either. Children were marginally more likely to be attached if contact was not thought desirable after placement (16 per cent, as compared with 58 per cent of those for whom contact was thought desirable). Interestingly, more children placed with siblings were well or fairly well attached (71 per cent, as compared with 53 per cent of those placed separately). Perhaps maintenance of the sibling relationship, by reducing a sense of being deserted, helps at the introduction stage and dilutes the demands made on any individual after placement. Children placed with a childless couple were more likely to be attached, but caution is needed here as the childless couples tended to take the younger children. If the parents either consented to adoption or were missing, the child was marginally less likely to be attached (63 per cent) than if the parents either did not consent or actively opposed adoption (72 per cent attached). Children who were behaviourally or emotionally disturbed when introduced to new families were less likely to be attached than those who were not disturbed, but at the two-year stage those who were behaviourally disturbed were more likely to be attached (54 per cent) than those who were emotionally disturbed (33 per cent attached). Previous attempts at permanence made no difference. For those who had, as for those who had not, previously attempted to join a new permanent family, 69 per cent were attached. If the new parents had picked out the child, the child was marginally more likely to be attached than if the child had been suggested to the new parents. Children who had been adopted or returned to a natural parent were more likely to be attached than those who hadn't but again this is closely related to age at placement, since none of the chilren over 12 at placement had been adopted. Even so, more than half the 14 foster children were at least fairly well attached.

WELL-BEING OF THE CHILDREN AFTER TWO YEARS

In considering the well-being of the 21 children still in the same placement after two years, we found some discrepancy between our sources of evidence. In 12 of the 17 cases where we had Rutter parent and teacher forms, the two sources agreed, but in five cases they differed. In two cases children whose behaviour at home was difficult were behaving well at school, but three of the five children who were assessed by teachers as showing marked disturbance were not rated by the parents as showing any disturbance.

On making comparisons with our assessment at referral, we found movement in both directions. Although two years after placement four children whose behaviour had been slightly disturbed were not showing signs of disturbance, two who had apparently not been disturbed were showing moderate disturbance, and one who had been only slightly disturbed was assessed as showing marked disturbance. For 11 there was no change; the behaviour of six had improved, and that of four had deteriorated.

We have already noted that difficult behaviour in the early stages of placement may be explained by the pressures children are under in trying to adjust to their new families, or understood as 'acting out' behaviour that, on the positive side, may bring the opportunity for closeness and thus help attachments to grow. By the two-year stage, however, any advantage to be gained from a temper tantrum or other piece of disturbed behaviour aimed at winning attention is likely to be offset by its negative effect on the new parents, depressed that the child should still feel so insecure as to find it necessary to behave in this way. Macaskill (1985) found such cases in her study of some difficult placements made by Parents for Children. The marked discrepancy in at least two cases between behaviour at home (reported as good) and behaviour at school (poor) may be explained by an extended 'honeymoon' period, or perhaps a fresh honeymoon period, with the children trying so hard to be on their best behaviour at home that they lost control at shcool. Alternatively, it may be that new parents were closing their eyes to the poor behaviour, trying to convince us or themselves that all was well, or had assumed that behaviour would be difficult and were therefore taking it in their stride. Several parents, after talking about difficulties they had had, said it wasn't half as bad as they had been led to expect.

For emotional as opposed to behavioural disturbance, as indicated by such symptoms as nervous habits or mannerisms, eating-problems, withdrawn behaviour, enuresis, psychosomatic symptoms, or excessively anxious or obsessional behaviour, we noted a different pattern. Whilst 13 children had shown signs of emotional disturbance at referral, only six showed any two years after placement, and change here was always in the direction of improvement. Whilst at the end of the study boys were still more likely to be behaviourally disturbed than girls, a third of the girls as opposed to only a quarter of the boys were seen as emotionally disturbed two years after placement. If there is validity in the argument that a degree of 'acting out' behaviour may help attachment, it may be that girls, whose problems are more likely to show themselves in the form of emotionally disturbed behaviour, may have more difficulty in becoming attached to new parents. This did not show up numerically, but some parents spoke of finding it more difficult to cope with withdrawal, sulkiness and what they described as 'deviousness' than with temper tantrums, running away and even stealing, which were more common amongst the boys. One mother said of her foster daughter,

She is damaged inside. That takes longer. She lies. Not bad lies – stupid lies. I ask her why and she just puts her head down and cries. It got to the stage where we were uncomfortable in the house. It felt at times that she was like a stuffed dummy and we wished she'd go to bed.

Just over half the 13 children placed who were behaviourally disturbed at the two-year stage were nevertheless either well attached or fairly well attached to parents, whereas four of the six who were emotionally disturbed were not considered to be even fairly well attached.

There was no change in intelligence as measured by the psychologist for any of the children, and changes in educational performance were mostly slight. The school performance of one teenager was much improved, and three other children had improved. 11 remained the same, and the educational performance of two children was worse. The reading attainment of one teenager as measured by the Wide Range Achievement Test had dropped from a standard score of 105 (above average) to 88, whilst a youngster of a similar age had improved his standard score on the same test from 60 to 74.

Using the reports available and our own observations we made an assessment of each child's well-being and progress or otherwise since placement or withdrawal from the project.

From tables 5.1 and 5.2 we see that the well-being of 23 children (81 per cent of those placed, and 75 per cent of those withdrawn) was considered to have improved since referral, and in no case was it considered to be worse. Nevertheless, the well-being of almost half the children in each group was still assessed as being below

Table 5.1 Well-being of children 18 months to two years after placement or withdrawal

	Children placed	Children withdrawn[a]	Total
Above average	6	0	6
Average	5	4	9
Below average	6	2	8
Poor	4	2	6
Total	21	8	29

[a] Current well-being of children withdrawn based on social workers' questionnaires.

Table 5.2 Well-being of children 18 months to two years after placement or withdrawal, as compared with well-being at time of referral

	Children placed	Children withdrawn[a]	Total
Much improved	5	2	7
Improved	12	4	16
Same	4	2	6
Worse	0	0	0
Total	21	8	29

[a] Current well-being of children withdrawn based on social workers' questionnaries.

average – a reminder that those who have experienced severe difficulties are not going to be miraculously cured when placed with a new family.

Finally, we made a general assessment of the success of each of the 22 placements made by the CWAH. Although only 15 families were involved, including the one from which a child was removed, our assessment of success was not necessarily the same for all siblings placed in the same home. We rated 13 placements as very successful and six as successful (an 86 per cent 'success' rate), but had reservations about two. Only one had failed. In assessing success, we not only considered the well-being of the children at the two-year stage, but also progress made. Thus placements where children were still rated as below average in terms of well-being might be rated as successful if a child was fairly well attached and had made progress. Equally, there might be reservations about the success of a placement where the child's well-being was good at placement and still good, but where there were indications of problems ahead, perhaps because of difficulties in coming to terms with the past.

We end this chapter by restating that 21 out of 22 placements (95 per cent) were successful in the sense that the child was still with the same family after two years, and that this is made even more remarkable by the fact that 71 per cent rated as showing some disturbance at referral and 34 per cent moderate or marked disturbance. The foster mother of a teenage boy commented,

The things that please me? The way he phones and says, 'Mum, I don't want you to worry – I am just round at Nick's place.' He tells you what he thinks. This life is great for him. His school report is a pleasure to read. He's not very bright but he tries. He was in the bottom class but he has pulled himself up to third from the bottom. He wasn't going to try at all when he came. He said it wasn't worth bothering to try.

SUMMARY

If success is measured by the rate of placement breakdown within two years, the project can boast a 95 per cent success rate. On a combination of other criteria, the researchers rated 86 per cent of the first 22 placements as successful. This does not mean that the children had, after two years with their new families, fully recovered from the damaging effects of earlier experiences. Older children, especially if they had not experienced earlier attachment to parent figures, had been abused or neglected or were maladjusted or institutionalized, were less likely to be attached to their new parents at the two-year stage, though some in each group had become attached. Half of those who had made previous attempts at permanent placement with substitute families were well or fairly well attached. 27 per cent of those referred (all but two of them aged over ten) were not placed by the project.

Two years after placement, all but one of the children over five when placed showed little sign of having improved their educational performance, and in some cases behaviour was more disturbed than at time of referral. Almost half the children – all under 12 at placement – had been adopted by the two-year stage. The well-being of almost half the children was still considered to be below average two years after placement. At the end of the study there were still question marks over an important minority of the children placed. Two years is too early to assess 'success' for older children placed with new parents. It is planned to interview the children and families again five years after placement.

6

The New Families

Richard came to stay with us for two weekends and we really liked him . . . but in my heart I knew I really wanted a baby and at fifteen he could never be that to me. . . . I felt I'd failed my husband, my daughter, Richard and the social workers. . . .

(Prospective adoptive mother)

We have a beautiful little baby girl whom we all love very much. Also a whole new lot of friends . . . we have entered a world we didn't know existed.

(Adoptive father)

In this chapter we consider some of the 521 couples and individuals who approached the CWAH in the hope of becoming adoptive or long-term foster parents. The journey towards the goal of offering a home to a child in need can be seen as a cycle encompassing rituals at various stages (see figure 3.1) The experiences of, and repercussions on, each family are unique to it. Yet, from a social work viewpoint, one can identify experiences and responses common to many families in facing the various hurdles along their journey.

As mentioned in chapter 3, the families have to attend a series of meetings and expose themselves 'publicly' to their referees and general practitioner, to social workers and the adoption panel, before they can be approved. The passage which the families have to travel in their search for a child may sometimes be an arduous and heart-breaking one. Some families only get as far as attending an inquirers' meeting, and realize, usually reasonably painlessly, that this type of adoption is not for them. One inquirer admitted,

'We learnt a lot about adopting handicapped children and I realized that I really wanted a healthy child.' Others set their hearts on individual children whose photographs they had seen on the office wall or in the 'Be My Parent' book, only to be 'counselled out' by the project worker or, in a few cases, 'declined' by the panel. One inquirer recalled, 'We set out hearts on a family of three children on the office wall, but the social worker said we would only be considered for the very hard-to-place child.' Another remembered, 'We wanted to give a handicapped baby a home and we liked one particular child in the 'Be My Parent' book. . . . When the panel turned us down we were very hurt.'

THE INQUIRY STAGE

A questionnaire was sent to each of the 115 couples and individuals who attended an open meeting between July 1980 and September 1982, and 75 (65 per cent) completed and returned the forms. Comparisons were made between the 14 'successful' families who still had a study child living with them two years after placement and the total group of respondents. Because we thought it important to reassure those completing questionnaires that they would not be identified, and questionnaires were sent out before we could know whether a child would be placed, we were unable to extract the replies of the case study families from the total sample. For this reason, and because the response rate of 65 per cent, although respectable for a postal questionnaire, is still quite low, comparisons can only be tentative.

Eight of the inquirers responding to the questionnaire (11 per cent) were single, as compared with only one of the successful applicants. We did not ask specifically about second marraiges, but have reason to conclude that there were a higher proportion of second marriage applicants in the total group than in the successful group. We know that three of the six potential new families actually turned down by the panel were couples where at least one partner had been married before (50 per cent, as compared with only 9 per cent – 5 out of 58 – of the family units approved by the panel). Questionnaire responses indicate that families where at least one partner has been previously married are an important source of applicants for older children in care or for sibling groups. Remarried couples, who are likely to be older and to have more advanced careers than first-marriage applicants, may see adoption or fostering as a means of having a child of the new marriage and may prefer to take an older child as likely to involve less disruption to careers and earning capacity than an infant. There was some 'case material' support for this hypothesis in our study, though our findings suggest that such applicants are more likely to be unsuccessful than are first-marriage applicants. For only one couple in our 'successful' case study group did the desire to have a child of the second marriage play a part in motivation. They did in fact separate in the course of the study, but the child was still well satisfied by the placement and has since been adopted by her new mother. In another successful family one of the parents had been married previously, and the single parent was a divorcee.

23 of the inquirers (31 per cent) were childless couples, and 52 (69 per cent) had children (five of whom were step-children). Of the case study families, four (28 per cent) were childless prior to their contact with the agency and ten (71 per cent) had children. Four of the 75 inquirers (6 per cent) had adopted before, and 14 (19 per cent) had fostered; the proportions are similar for the case study group (one had adopted and three had fostered previously). 27 of the inquirers (33 per cent) had unsuccessfully applied to become adoptive or long-term foster parents through another agency, and 20 (27 per cent) were still in contact with another adoption agency, whilst two of the case study group had applied to another agency and had been turned down, and others had made tentative inquiries but had been put off by what they saw as a lukewarm or negative response.

Handicapped babies, sibling groups, black or mixed race children and older children were the most-sought-after categories of children, and the number of inquirers interested was roughly the same for each category. However, only six said they wanted a physically handicapped older child, and only three a mentally handicapped older child.

It is interesting to note that a higher proportion of older children (those over the age of seven) were placed than was originally envisaged by the initial inquirers. One inquirer stated, 'We'd heard that there were lots of "battered toddlers" who needed good homes but most of the children this agency had to offer were older than we had in mind. . . .'

About a quarter of the respondents had had experience of children with special needs; 12 had worked with children with behaviour difficulties and six said they had had to contend with the behaviour problems of one of their own children. Six had worked with physically handicapped children and three had physically handicapped children of their own. Only two had worked with children in care. Two inquirers stated that they were looking after step-children and felt that these were also children with special needs.

In the case study group, three families had experience of mentally handicapped childrren: one couple had a Down's syndrome child of their own, and two were fostering mentally handicapped teenagers. The only other people to have experience of children with special needs were two couples who had previously fostered older children and an adoptive mother who had worked with children in care.

Inquirers were asked to indicate on a check list their main and secondary reasons for wishing to foster or adopt. 32 (43 per cent) gave 'wish to give a home to a child in need' as their first reason, and 21 gave it as their second reason. One inquirer commented, 'We hated the idea of handicapped children being left in institutions, and we wanted to give them the support and love they need.' A similar number (34) gave as their main reason the satisfaction of a need of their own (to have a child of their own or to add to their families, where it was difficult or impossible to achieve this themselves). 14 gave this as their second reason. One respondent stated, 'We have one child and are not able to have any more but we feel we could offer a home to a child and give our own son a much wanted brother or sister. . . .' 'Really enjoy being with children' was the major reason for only nine inquirers, but was the most frequently ticked secondary reason (25).

All except two of the successful group gave 'wish to give a home to a child in need' or 'really enjoy being with children' as their first or second reason. Of the two others, one gave 'difficulties in having a child of their own' and the other 'companion for own child' as the main reason. Motivation is a complex subject to which we return in the next chapter.

48 (57 per cent) of the inquirers said they wanted to adopt a child and 18 (24 per cent) that they wanted to foster on a long-term basis with a view to adoption. A further eight inquirers (11 per cent) stated that they wanted to foster a child on a long-term basis, and the remaining 8 per cent had no preference. In the case study group, seven couples (50 per cent) have adopted, five (36 per cent) are fostering with a view to adoption, and two (14 per cent) are long-term foster parents.

Some inquirers were annoyed that so much emphasis was placed on intention to adopt, especially by the local authority workers:

> We wanted to offer a child a home but we weren't in the initial stages prepared to commit ourselves to adoption . . . the social worker told us we didn't stand a chance unless we intended to adopt. . . .

> I wanted to adopt eventually but I felt it would be right to foster a child first and adopt only if we were all sure it was the right thing. I didn't want to commit myself or my husband to adopting an older child right from the start as I felt the agency wanted.

THE 'PREPARATION' STAGE

Inquirers who after the open meeting were still interested in parenting a 'hard-to-place' child were visited by one of the social workers and attended a course of four evening meetings or two evening meetings and an extended Saturday session. These meetings included films, talks by the social workers, discussion and talks by 'veteran' adoptive or foster parents. The purpose of the initial home visit was to 'counsel out' totally inappropriate inquiries and to give some encouragement to potentially suitable inquirers to continue towards their goal of fostering or adopting.

These comments represent a cross-section of reasons given by respondents who did not pursue their inquiry beyond this stage:

> At the initial inquiry we stated that we have children and that we both worked. It was said at the time that this made no difference and we were invited to attend their open day. However, these have been the reasons for them stating that we don't take our application further . . . after wasting our time by insisting that we attend their lecture. . . .

> We feel much clearer now about the whole concept of the placement of hard-to-place children. . . . We do not however feel that we are settled enough in our own life to be suitable for this type of commitment.

> At the beginning we understood there would be details and photographs of about 15 children needing permanent homes. At the open meeting we found the number much less than this. . . . We had been hoping to be drawn to a particular child but the turnover was not great. . . . We have not pursued our inquiry as we got the feeling that if you are childless in this county and want to adopt, you don't stand much chance.

18 of the 75 respondents (24 per cent) either withdrew or were 'counselled out' by a project worker at the inquiry stage.

Most respondents who gave details about why they decided not to proceed with an application after attending a preparation group said that they felt that the agency was not offering the sort of child they had in mind, even though they found the social workers themselves very helpful. One respondent wrote, 'The children were all much more handicapped than we had imagined. We felt sure there must be healthy children elsewhere needing homes.' A few, however, felt that 'The whole process was too long-winded', and one inquirer commented, 'We've fostered literally dozens of children in London and it's never taken as long as this to get a child. . . .'

There were no obvious differences between those who attended preparation groups and those who merely attended an inquirers' meeting. It may well be that the main difference was a determination on the part of the former group to proceed with this particular agency.

Only 25 (33 per cent) of the questionnaire respondents went on to attend preparation groups during the research period, and 19 of these (76 per cent) stated that they felt they were expected to attend these meetings. In addition, whilst 20 (80 per cent) felt hopeful that they would be able to foster or adopt through the agency, only ten (33 per cent) were approved by the panel during the study period.

The following comments are representative of the replies of respondents who dropped out during or after attending preparation groups. One commented,

After attending the preparation groups we became more aware of the problems involved and I of my own ability. We were told we would have to limit ourselves to adopting an older teenager but I feel more suited to younger children, so we did not pursue our inquiry.

Others felt that their own spouse, children or relatives did not support them:

We didn't begin to think of our own little boy's feelings until we attended the preparation groups. When we did ask his feelings he said he didn't want a black or handicapped brother and we knew this was the only type of child we would get.

We didn't tell relatives about our plans until after we'd attended the meetings. We experienced a lot of opposition from relatives, especially older generations, to our plans. It caused friction and we realized another child would not easily be accepted. . . .

After we'd attended the meetings at The Child Wants a Home, we realized that, although I wanted to foster a handicapped child, my husband did not. . . . We felt we both had to agree on the type of child. . . .

Others were put off by the social worker's response:

We were told we were too old after we'd attended the meetings, so we went and got in touch with our local social services. . . . We're very pleased as we are now fostering a little boy and girl. . . .

THE APPLICATION STAGE

All the families who got through this stage successfully felt that it was necessary, albeit lengthy and time-consuming. Applicants were asked to fill in a detailed application form and undergo a medical examination; checks were made with police, social services, health and probation departments; and references were taken up and referees interviewed. At the same time the family's worker visited them regularly, interviewing all members of the family and perhaps making suggestions about children they might be interested in and ways in which they might improve their knowledge of children with particular problems. The following are some comments on this stage:

It seemed to take ages and they were very thorough; even though we expected this it was often an inconvenience at the time.

We felt very vulnerable at this stage . . . we knew we had to keep in the social worker's good books or she wouldn't recommend us to the panel.

They really went into our past very thoroughly. . . . I think we came out of it feeling we knew ourselves better and we were lucky as we got approved. . . . I can imagine you don't feel so positive about it if you are rejected by the panel. . . .

Seven families said (and the agency's records agree) that they were declined or counselled out by the project worker in the later stages of the home study and therefore did not get as far as the panel, whilst only three families were formally declined by the panel itself. This distinction is important for some families in coming to terms with the reasons why they were not regarded by this agency as suitable to foster or adopt. Being 'counselled out' appeared to create less resentment than being formally declined. Reasons why families were turned down or 'counselled out' included social isolation, a husband's police record and problems in the marriage. Only one family was declined solely on the basis of medical reports, although several families who eventually fostered or adopted through the project had been turned down by others on the basis of ill health.

17 families were turned down or counselled out at this final stage, and comments indicated sadness or bitterness with the social workers:

We felt put out by specious excuses . . . we didn't get on with the social worker.

We were told that the rules of assessment were unbending and the panel's decision final. I felt that I was seen as unfit rather than unsuitable. . . .

We were told that our house was too tidy for their kind of children . . . they could have told us that much earlier on.

We felt the agency had taken an unrealistic and old-maidish approach. . . .

FAMILIES WHO WERE APPROVED BY THE PANEL

In seven cases, families approved by the agency were introduced to a child but the introduction broke down and the families were discouraged from proceeding with further introductions. This was possibly the hardest blow that any of the rejected families had to bear, as those in question had been so close to getting the child they had wished for. Four of these families agreed to be interviewed, and the following are some of their comments:

We felt bitter towards the local authority social worker for giving us an emotionally disturbed child when we didn't ask for one.

We really liked the child but the agency said he wasn't right for us. . . . We were all disappointed.

We were accepted as adoptive parents and progressed to meetings with the child. . . . Alas, although we feel she accepted us, she just could not 'fly the nest'. It was a case of the right family and the right child had come together two years too late and it left us feeling very sad.

We could identify no obvious differences between the families where introductions failed and those which constitute the case study group.

The following comments about the application process are representative of those made by families who were approved and either had a child placed with them or were waiting for a child to be placed:

What was only a possibility now is becoming a reality. We got tremendous help from all the staff. It is the fulfilment of a long awaited dream. . . .

We have learned a lot about the needs of these children and made friends with the social worker. (Previously we had little respect for social workers.) We are now pleased to say that we shall soon have a child to share our home with. . . .

FAMILIES WITH WHOM A STUDY CHILD WAS SUCCESSFULLY PLACED

The 27 new parents ranged in age from 33 to 60. 14 were aged between 30 and 40; 11 between 40 and 50. The 14 families consisted of 13 married couples and one single woman. All the parents were white and were British subjects.

The social class of the families as defined by the Registrar General's classification of occupations ranged from class one to class 5. All except two families were in social class 3 (clerical or skilled manual) or 5 (unskilled manual).

In only four cases were both parents working. Occupations included cook, teacher, university lecturer, trained nurse, post-mistress, engineer and small businessman. One father had retired early because of ill health. Eight of the families were earning £5,500 a year or less at application, which indicates that on the whole this group were earning less than the national average, even though they were in the middle in terms of social class. Seven of the parents had higher educational qualifications, even though they were not in employment which required these qualifications: one draughtsman, for example, took up unskilled employment after redundancy. We considered it to be of interest that, at a time of high unemployment, none was unemployed for more than a brief period of time. The determination to be in work, even if at a lower level than that for which the person in question was qualified, fits with the tendency towards self-reliance which we note below.

The religious affiliations of families included Methodist, Baptist, Church of England and Christian Scientist. Four of the families were churchgoers and one opted for the description 'religious, but not churchgoers'. The other ten families did not attend church regularly and did not see themselves as having any particular religious faith.

In only two cases was there a second marriage, and in a third case the single parent was a divorcee. 13 of the 14 new families were made up of married couples, nine of whom had children of their own (including one with an adopted child of a previous marriage). The other family consisted of a single parent with grown-up children of a previous marriage. Between them, the families had 28 children of their own in addition to their adopted or foster children, and all the children, apart from five who were grown up, still lived with their parents. Some of the parents had experienced the loss of a child through adoption or still-birth or because the child had remained with a previous marriage partner. None of the families had any extended family living in their homes, although five lived very close to other relatives.

All except two were owner occupiers. The other two families lived in council houses and both were overcrowded following the arrival of the new children. Six of the families lived in towns and the other eight in rural areas.

Six of the new parents had ill health of some nature, such as arthritis, diabetes, high blood pressure or hormone problems. These were all diagnosed before the children were placed and did not prevent the parents from being judged medically fit to foster or adopt. Only one of these parents could be said to be in poor physical health, but in this case his wife was considered fit enough to foster single-handed if her husband's health should take a turn for the worse.

Ten families had no fertility problems; two couples were childless owing to male infertility and one owing to female infertility; and the remaining couple had been advised against having their own children after the death of their first baby. The four childless couples all said that they were consoled by the fact that they were approved to adopt children:

We didn't like babies anyway . . . we prefer older children.

We didn't think there were any babies for adoption these days and heard that you can adopt brothers and sisters, which is what we wanted.

One couple, however, were still saddened by the fact that they couldn't have their 'own' baby and when applying to the agency asked for 'a child as young as possible'.

Only two of these families had 'done the rounds' of the baby adoption agencies. One couple were turned down on medical grounds and the other approved to adopt a white, healthy baby but, 'after we were told we might have to wait up to five years for a child, we decided to try for older children in the hope that we would get our family sooner'.

Most of the new parents said that their own childhoods had been strict but predominantly happy and most had been largely conformist as teenagers. However, in seven of the 14 families at least one parent had suffered the death of a mother or father during childhood, and five of these parents had been fostered or looked after by relatives. One had been in residential care, and another had been in custody as a teenager. In some of the other seven families, one of the partners described difficult relations with parents and said that this had given an incentive to be a 'better parent', both to his or her own children and to 'someone else's child'.

Three of the new families had fostered before and most of the others had looked after their own or other people's children either as childminders, as 'social aunts and uncles' to children in care, or as aunts and uncles to large families. None of the families had had no experience with 'ordinary' children. One adoptive mother had previously worked with handicapped children and another family had a handicapped child of their own.

We spent some time during our interviews with the case study families in discussing their values and their attitudes to family life and relationships. We also had access to the project workers' detailed reports. The majority of families appeared as warm, conformist, family-centred, believing in self-reliance, holding strongly to their own beliefs and able to talk about their worries. Marriage partners tended to have differentiated sex roles, but to take decision jointly and to draw emotional support mainly from each other.

We are doers in this family. We don't sit back and do nothing and just talk. We get on and do something.

In our democratic family the children and adults discuss things. We don't bottle things up, and go round slamming doors. But in the end the adults make the decisions.

In terms of child care, most of the families were fairly strict and used physical punishment, but also had a great deal of positive physical contact with their children through kissing and cuddling. One parent said, 'I could have taken any child – if I knew they needed something', while another commented,

If you take on something as tricky as this you have to do what comes naturally. You can't always be watching your reactions. If you are a 'slapper', you can't think constantly – you won't survive if you are thinking: I mustn't hit foster children. I'm not advocating slapping, but it's better a quick slap than brooding.

The main characteristics which united these families, who were in many respects so different, were their enjoyment of being with children, their individualism and determination. The following comments give a flavour of the way they described themselves:

I would apply again. Even though it has been very hard. I don't think they would put me off. I can't imagine not having children around.

The thing is, we are a very independent family. We don't rely on anyone – in-laws, out-laws or anyone else. We stand on our own two feet.

I have promised his sisters that I will carry it through – keeping him in touch with them and his family. And I will carry it through if it kills me.

As all the families agreed, the journeys they had started on were long, strenuous and often emotional. Hurdles had to be negotiated at every stage. Many families' lives changed simply as a result of the application and assessment process, let alone the events surrounding the actual placement of a child. Yet, as we show in the next chapter, most of those who persisted and overcame what some saw as the necessary and others as the vexatious obstacles placed in the way of their acceptance as parents of 'hard-to-place' children were glad that they had had those experiences, and most of those with whom a child was actually placed found the process, as one foster father commented, 'a most rewarding experience which has taught [us] a great deal about ourselves and about children with special needs'. A foster mother gave the following tip: 'You've got to be determined to see it through . . . you need patience and willpower to keep going. . . .'

SUMMARY

The range of families offering to provide permanent homes to children with special needs is wide. 'Successful' families included those with and those without children of their own; those who had previously fostered or adopted and those who had not; members of all social classes; those whose lives had been happy and uneventful, and those who had had to cope with ill health, stress and unhappiness in their own lives; those who were principally motivated by self-interest, and those whose motivation was mainly altruistic.

Characteristics often found amongst successful families were as follows: really enjoying being with children; having some experience of children with special needs; being family-centred and having a strong marriage; believing in self-reliance; being tolerant of others but firmly holding fairly conventional views about how their own lives should be lived; being fairly relaxed about achievement, talking about worries and problems rather than internalizing them. If married, they tended to have well differentiated sex roles. They tended to be strict with their children and, if the occasion merited it, to use physical punishment, but also to have a lot of positive physical contact with them. It should be said, though, that some successful families differed markedly from the majority in all these respects. One of the characteristics which these families all shared – persistence which at times bordered on stubbornness – obviously contributed to success in that they determinedly pursued their objective of taking a hard-to-place child and refused to be put off by delays or discouraging comments by family, friends or social workers.

7

The New Families after Placement

I thought after six months and then after a year that the children were settled, and then every so often we'd have an upset, and I wondered if they'd ever settle down. Then at two years I thought they'd got better. The last six months have been the best. We still have bad times, like any family, but I'm really glad we had them. Fostering's like married life, you have to take the rough with the smooth.

(Foster mother of two teenagers)

RECONSTITUTED FAMILIES

The situation of the adoptive families after children had been placed with them in many ways echoed that of the 'reconstituted' or 'blended' family (Burgoyne and Clark, 1982; Rimmer, 1983) after divorce and remarriage. After a transitional period when the family constitution changes to accommodate its new members, the complex relationships which are inherent within any nuclear family assume even greater complexity in adoptive and in step-families. Couples become new parents; natural children of the family gain new siblings; the new child gains new mother and father figures and possibly a number of new siblings, and usually a new set of grandparents, aunts, uncles and cousins.

Burgoyne and Clark (1982) suggest that it is helpful to consider the issues facing reconstituted families in two ways: the dominant concern is with the practical and the material, with 'concrete matters' such as housing and income and, more specifically, questions about access and parenting someone else's children; in addition there are the problems of how people make sense of the process of reconstitution – how they explain what has happened to them and how they incorporate new parental and marital feelings and experiences into their lives.

In this study, the parallels between adoptive families and step-families are immediately obvious, since many of the families had their own children before adopting or fostering, and most of the older children placed had had some contacts with their birth families before placement. The new families encountered both practical problems to do with parenting someone else's (often handicapped) child and emotional difficulties to do with the clash between their expectations and their actual experiences of what adoption entails.

In adoptive and reconstituted families there are also some problems about the collective identity of the family to ousiders, where some members are not readily identifiable as part of the family. Differnces of surname may cause embarrassement at school, which is why some older children in our study changed their surnames almost immediately on placement. But children whose physical appearance (for instance, skin or hair colour) was markedly different from that of other family members were obliged to find a 'cover story' – an answer to questions about their origins with which they were more or less comfortable and which would be upheld by other members of the family.

Thus, for the individual members of an adoptive or step-family, attempts to create an 'ideal' nuclear unit may be hampered by conflicts between expectations and experiences and exacerbated by obvious differences of identity between a new child and other family members. The process of integration is further complicated by the mixture of feelings which different family members may have at any one time. On the one hand, there may be the sense of loss of a natural parent, coupled with jealousy at having to share parents with a new child; on the other hand, new children may feel that because they were not born into the family, their new parents feel less for them than for those who were and that this affects how they are treated.

It must, however, be stressed that, whilst adoptive families have their problems, they should not be seen as 'problem' families. For many of the families in our study, adopting a child or children with special needs was regarded as the 'most rewarding thing' they had ever done, the realization of a much-wished-for family life.

There were 14 families in the main case study group, and one in which the placement broke down after two months. In the analysis in this chapter, all 15 families are included unless otherwise stated. Between them the 15 families had 30 children of their own: one family had five children; two families had four children; three had three children; three had two children; two had one child; and there were four childless couples. After placement two families had six children, two had five, two had four, three had three, four had two, and two had one. Thus more than half had three or more children. Of the total number of 51 children, 25 were fostered or adopted and 26 were 'own' children.

GETTING TO KNOW EACH OTHER

The introductory period varied in length and nature, and dependend on the age of the child, the previous placement and distance from it, and the willingness of previous caretakers to give time and even accommodation to the new parents. Other considerations were the social workers' perceptions of the stress on the children of looking in separate directions at once, especially if they were attached to those they were living with; and pressures of time where the previous foster parents were moving, a children's home was closing down or the child needed to start a new school at the start of term. Some new parents thought that not enough attention was given to the stress on them, and their own children, of travelling long distances and having their routines disrupted; they felt that, because everyone was exhausted, placements got off to a bad start.

The length of introduction was different in each case but in none exceeded six months. For the younger children it tended to be between one and two months; for the older ones, between three and four. For each of the toddlers, the new family visited the child's previous home two or three times, usually staying in the short-term foster home for up to a week and during this time gradually taking over care of the child. With older and handicapped children, the introductory period usually involved the new families making a daytime or overnight visit to the previous home to meet them and those who were caring for them. In one case where a considerable distance was involved, the parents moved into the children's home for a week and then took the children, aged four and three, back with them. In most cases the initial visit was tense and artificial.

A small minority of families asked for a 'blind viewing' – the opportunity of seeing children without their being aware of it – but these situations created tense moments and had to be carefully stage-managed. One mother recalled, 'We followed the children round the museum. We kept looking at them and wanting to take them home there and then. The social worker said we had to call the blind viewing off because she thought the children had noticed we were watching them.' We have already noted that in the permanent placement of older children 'chemistry' plays an important part, and for some families 'blind viewing' was important in helping them make up their minds. Some of the local authority workers we spoke to and some of the new parents were critical of this practice, to the extent of finding it distasteful, but one at least of the most successful placements started in this way, although the only placement which was disrupted also started with a 'blind viewing'.

For other families a picture of the child was enough. One family decided on the basis of a newspaper article that Eddy was the boy they would like to take into their home, and having made their decision, there was absolutely no point in their seeing him to make sure. In the eight months or so until a meeting did take place, they became attached to him without having even seen him, and they described vividly to us how they had thought about him on his birthday and felt impotently angry at the delay, which meant that he was getting older and precious time being wasted.

If the initial visit went well enough, and the new parents, children and both social workers thought it appropriate to proceed, the older children would visit for days and then weekends. During this time, tension was often ventilated as anger against the local authority for failing to provide material goods, or for insisting on what some parents felt was an unnecessarily long introductory period or an unnecessary bureaucratic procedure. One father complained, 'The social services department left everything to the last minute. The children were arriving within twenty-four hours and we still hadn't got any beds.' The older children met their new families between two and eight times before moving in, but for most the number of meetings was about six.

'TRIAL MARRIAGE' VERSUS 'ARRANGED MARRIAGE'

In conducting our interviews we were made aware of the similarities between fostering an older child for a while before adopting, and living together before marriage (or 'trial marriage'). For older children and their new families, fostering provides an important opportunity for getting to know each other before making the permanent commitment of adoption. The children are able to test out their readiness to give up or weaken their ties to their families of origin, and their ability to give themselves emotionally to their new families. The new families may also see this as an important period in which to weigh up their feelings towards their foster children and to decide whether or not they really do wish to make the child their own in the eyes of the law. As one family said, 'We felt pressure from the social workers to adopt the children from the word "go" . . . but we knew we needed six months to sort out our feelings and decide if adoption was right for us.' Another foster mother felt it was only after having the children for two years that she was even ready to consider 'the commitment of adoption'. She also felt that she wanted the satisfaction of knowing she could call on her social worker for support when necessary, and saw this as an advantage of fostering which was denied to adopters.

Not all new families or children see adoption as a necessary step, a point explored fully by Rowe and her colleagues (1984). For some in our study, financial difficulties prevented them from applying to adopt at the time, but they saw adoption as a desirable step for themselves and the children before they left school: 'The children know we want to adopt them, but it will take a long time before we can afford it.' This father felt custodianship would make a difference but added, 'We'd still want adoption . . . it's more secure.' Adoption allowances were not available when these placements were made.

Others wanted to adopt as soon as possible and could not really feel free from anxiety until after the hearing. As one father said, 'I did feel more secure once the order was made.' Relationships in another family improved dramatically after the adoption, as the parents relaxed and allowed themselves to be more natural with a six-year-old and he sensed the reduction of tension. These parents said they needed to adopt in order to get rid of what they saw as the burden of people telling them how to do things. The mother insisted, 'We can't establish what we think is right for Peter if some outside person is having a say.'

For others, adoption was not seen as appropriate at all. One foster mother said, 'We don't think Andrew needs adoption . . . he's got a real mum and dad who he sees and he knows we're not his real mum and dad.' Thus, whilst for many of the families in this study adoption offered a security akin to that offered by marriage – both parties joined in law – this was by no means the view of all the families, and, as we saw in chapter 5, fewer than half had been legally adopted at the two-year stage.

Whether a child was fostered or adopted did not appear to have much impact on the satisfaction of most of the parents. However, not being adopted caused problems for some *children* who had come to feel that only adoption could provide security, and who made the move in the expectation of being adopted. Compared to the children placed for adoption, those placed as foster children where there was no intention to adopt settled as well and were assessed as being as successfully placed. The analogy must surely be with a promise of marriage which is later retracted. 'Living together' may now be a fashionable alternative to marriage for some adults, but for a child a promise is a promise. As one foster father commented, 'Security for ourselves and for the children would make adoption preferable. But you have to put that at the back of your mind and get on with it. Dave wants adoption to get rid of social workers and to be normal.'

As a general rule, we found that adoption became less necessary to the parents as they realized that there was not the slightest possibility of the children being taken away unless they or the children asked for it. Adoption, they felt, would not make any difference, since they had already demonstrated how determined they were to make the placement work. On the other hand, two children, when asked if they had three wishes, put adoption at the top of their list. Partly this was in order to be 'normal' and partly as a further guarantee against being sent away. More importantly, though, for at least two children who had been subjected to several moves, adoption was seen as a sign that they were the sort of people who were sufficiently lovable to be adopted. Sadly, although money was one of the reasons why they had not been adopted, we saw indications that a more important reason was that their new parents or siblings had not yet convinced themselves that they *were* sufficiently 'lovable' or had adapted sufficiently well to become full members of the families in the legal sense implied by adoption. One father who had originally intended to adopt said, 'Till I get them sorted out, I don't want them to take our name.'

CONTACT WITH PEOPLE FROM THE CHILDREN'S PAST

The willingness of the new family to meet the child's natural family varied greatly. In five cases (nine children) the natural parents had met the new family before placement. These meetings had all taken place in the local authority social worker's office. In each case, the new parents said they had found the meeting helpful and considered it positive to the natural parents and the child that they had met. As one adoptive father remarked, 'I'm glad we met the children's mother. I think it put her mind at rest and it was good for the children to know we'd met her.' One new mother, however, commented that the meetings, which had started before placement and continued afterwards, involved 'hassle over travelling and the [natural] family often get uptight. . . . Sometimes I'd like to move to Scotland to be out of the way . . . but the meetings mean so much to Martin and his sisters and grandparents . . . we have to continue for their sakes. . . .'

After placement only two families continued to meet their foster child's natural parents (though in two cases the natural father rang the foster parents occasionally). In both cases visits took place about once every three months. The new parents said they 'quite enjoyed' seeing their children's birth parents and knew it was helpful to the children: 'It's very helpful to Dan that we will let him see his mother whenever he and she want a meeting. His mother is as much a mystery to him as she is to us; he seems to feel safe with us.'

In two of the five cases where the new family had met the natural family before placement, there was continued contact with the child's siblings and, in one case, also grandparents and an aunt. One adoptive father commented, 'Paul doesn't worry about seeing his sisters because he knows he's going to see them. . . . We made a commitment to keep him in contact with his family . . . so he can get on with settling in to our family. . . .'

However, visiting a child's relatives could create considerable difficulties for the new parents. Long distances might be involved, and, to pass the time till the child was ready to come home, parents might for instance take their own children to the zoo, which would be very expensive. One mother remarked, 'We spend a fortune on our children when we take Paul to see his family. We drop him off with them and come back for him at the end of the day, which means we have to amuse ourselves while we're waiting.'

Sometimes families played host for a week at a time to their foster children's natural siblings; the need 'to be polite while tempers are frayed' often created strains on family members in already overcrowded households. One family had the problem that their foster child's natural family were often critical of their care of the child and sent him expensive presents, such as a television, whilst ignoring the new family's own children.

Although contact created some problems for the new families, they stressed that this contact had a positive value for the children. One father remarked, 'Before the visit to his sisters he is all eager. He talks a lot of codswallop on the way there in the car because he's so excited.'

Two families welcomed the regular but infrequent visits of, in the one case, the natural parents, and, in the other, the mother and siblings. In the latter case the foster mother said of the natural mother:

I find her a simple, pleasant soul. Not much different from them [her children] in some ways. The first time she came Philip was a bit disturbed. She had a new flat. He asked her if he could go back with her and she said no. He was pretty disturbed by that but he soon got over it. He was disturbed for the first two times she came but last time she came he didn't play much attention.

For most of the families referred to above, limited contact with the natural family after placement was seen as desirable for the child and, because of this, acceptable to the new family. However, only one foster mother actually said she positively enjoyed regular contact with her foster child's natural parent. This placement was regarded by the researchers as the most inclusive (Holman, 1972) arrangement, with foster parents, children and, as far as was known, natural parent in favour of continuing contact.

Most of the 15 case study families were accepting of the children's backgrounds inasmuch as they did not deny them opportunities to talk about their past. However, most families were much more wary of actual contact with natural parents, even when restricted to letters. Although happy to send a photo to their adopted daughter's parents, one mother commented, 'I don't want contact with them. If they came down here they would be looking at how we were bringing her up.'

Others believed in the 'fresh start' approach, but were not 'exclusive' in the sense of being unwilling to accept or talk about the children's previous lives. One adoptive mother noted that 'The children really opened up after they did their life story work; now they've put the past behind them and we never talk about it.'

In another case the two eldest children of a sibling group corresponded with their mother for a while, but this contact was ended, partly because the new parents felt it was impeding the process of attachment. The foster mother commented,

With the younger children it was better to have made the break . . . they are very confused. Mike doesn't talk about his mother but I have a feeling he will look her up in the future. . . . Jenny wrote to her mother and said she belonged here and that her mother was being unfair . . . it wasn't until after that that the children started to let themselves go with us. . . .

Mike did later resume contact with his natural mother. Only one family discouraged any discussion of the child's early life, although four more didn't initiate discussion and felt some discomfort when the subject was brought up.

Contact between the new families and the child's previous caretakers was limited. It is the policy of the CWAH to introduce each family to the child's residential worker or foster parents before placement and to encourage them to take a major part in the introductory process. In most cases contact after placement is expected to tail off fairly quickly and in only one case was it anticipated that a child and his new family would keep in contact with a previous house parent who was also the child's godparent. Sadly, as so often happens, the child in question became angry with his well-intentioned godmother (who decided not to visit until she felt he had settled in). We considered that this was a case where Bowlby's theories of attachment and loss (Bowlby, 1971) were relevant, and misunderstanding of the child's reaction when visited by the person who had cared for him led to the loss of a relationship which was important to him and could have continued to be so. What was originally envisaged as frequent contact by the child's houseparent became very infrequent after placement. The foster mother said, 'Martin says he hates Carol and tries to shut her off . . . he wants to shut the past out of his mind. . . .'

THE DEVELOPMENT OF ATTACHMENT

In chapter 1 we referred to the trend towards avoiding 'drift' for children in care by placing them with permanent substitute families. Behind this trend lies the view that, for satisfactory adjustment in adult life, especially in a society where the nuclear family is still the favoured way of living and of bringing up children, it is essential for a child to experience the positives but also the demands which come from being loved and nurtured by a caring adult – that is, from being 'attached' to a 'psychological' parent, who may or may not be the birth parent. Thus the major benefit to be hoped for from 'permanence' is 'attachment' – the experience of loving and being loved by parents, making it easier to love and to accept love, to trust and to be trusted, in adult life. If a child does not become attached, should we consider that the permanent placement has been unsuccessful, or are there other benefits of permanence on which judgements of success should be based? The view has been expressed by the Barnardo's team in Glasgow (Fallon et al., 1983) that for some older children a more appropriate if more modest aim should be to provide security, continuity and the opportunity to be cared about as part of a family. Also, can attachment be one-way, or must it be mutual to be of benefit? We raise these questions to counteract a rather simplisitic notion of 'bonding' which comes across in some of the literature. When we talked to the parents and children about the growth of attachment and tried to assess whether and when a child should be considered 'attached' to a new family, we were obliged to take account of the multi-faceted nature of attachment: child to mother; child to father; mother to child; father to child; child to each sibling; each sibling to child.

There was wide variation in the time it took for the children to become attached to their new families and for different family members to become attached to each child. One new mother observed, 'There was no doubt in my mind, they were looking for a dad, more than they were looking for a mum. But I was prepared to wait, no matter how long it took. It is not something you can force on them.' There was also variation within sibling groups in terms of the development of attachment. In a family of three siblings, the youngest child, who had spent only a short period in a family setting, became attached to his new family, and they to him, in a matter of weeks. However, his older sister was seen as being only marginally attached to the new family at the end of the two-years period. All the parents of the younger children said they had formed close mutual attachments within the first three months; the same had happend with a seven-year-old child. Five of the eight other children aged between five and ten were considered to have become attached by six months after placement, and the other three by the one-year stage. However, in four of these eight cases, at least one member of the new family was seen as not attached to the child by the one-year stage. It should be noted that especially for younger children we were heavily dependent on the opinions of parents about when the child had become attached to them, although the psychologist's and social worker's reports were also considered. It may be that parents assumed that the child's feelings for them were the same as theirs for the child and underestimated the time it took for their feelings to be reciprocated.

Two of the nine children aged 11 or over were seen as attached to their families by the three-months stage, although in both cases not all members of the new family felt attached to the child. A foster father explained the diversity of affections within his family as 'partly jealousy' and the fact that his older children had got to an age when they didn't 'want to share us with any others'. In the four cases where natural children took longer to accept the new child as part of the family, this caused considerable heartache. For a further four children in this age group it took a year or more for them to become attached to their new families and the families to them, whilst four children were felt to be poorly attached to their new families two years after placement.

Some new parents would only allow themselves to feel attached to the child when they felt the child was attached to them and *vice versa*. The following comments were offered by two mothers:

In spite of everything, he's always made it clear he wanted to be here.

He tells his mates how much he loves us. He says, 'Oh mum, that dinner was lovely, thank you mum.' I enjoy doing things for him.

Parents inevitably compared their feelings towards the newcomers with their feelings towards children born to them, some being of the opinion that the nature of the attachment was the same from a very early stage, others feeling either that it took longer really to love the new child, or that the nature or degree of attachment was different. One mother said about her new six-year-old son, one year after placement, 'I still don't feel the same towards Peter as I do towards Amy. Sometimes he drives me up the wall, and I find him irritating. . . . It's getting better, but I had a romantic view of adoption, and it's like forcing yourself to love a stranger.' In contrast, a father said of a Down's toddler, 'Never has there been a time when she seemed like someone else's child. You kiss her on the lips, and think nothing of it.' He said he reazlied he had accepted his new daughter as part of the family when he found himself licking the spoon he had just been using to feed her.

Other parents found they became attached to one sibling as if he had been born to them but not to another. Three years after placement one foster mother confessed,

One day Sam said, 'I don't behave like you want me to behave. I'll have to go back.' I knew he didn't mean it. He wanted me to talk and sit down and give him attention. It's more inside. He wants to get at you. He was throwing it back in my face. I felt I'd failed him. He is so good in some ways, but I can't really trust him. I can let myself go with Jim, you know, lose my temper. But I never have to. I consider him part of the family. Well, I do with Sam up to a point. Jim, I can treat him just the same as my others. Sam, no. I have to walk away. It shouldn't be so. After 18 months, that was really bad, and then again at about two years. For the last three months it hasn't been so bad.

MATCHING NEED AND MOTIVATION

Much has been written in the professional literature about the importance of motivation to the success or otherwise of foster or adoptive placements. Most practitioners consider a thorough examination of the reasons which lie behind the offer of a home to be crucial to the assessment and matching process. More recently writers have cast doubt on this view (Shaw and Hipgrave, 1983). We noted in chapter 6 that the stated reason for offering a home to a 'hard-to-place' child tended to be either child-centred or new-family-centred, but that 'really enjoying being with children' was an important second reason for almost all in each group. Table 7.1 lists the number of times the different reasons were mentioned by the new families interviewed. Most applicants mentioned three or four reasons which combined altruism and self-interest, though usually one or other was dominant. One family mentioned seven different reasons, and two mentioned only two – in one case both family-centred, in the other both altruistic. It should be noted that there was no apparent difference in success between those whose reasons were mainly self-directed and those where they were mainly child-directed.

In our discussions with the families about their satisfactions and

Table 7.1 Reasons given by 15 case study families for offering a home to a 'hard-to-place' child

Reason	Number of times mentioned
To become parents	5
To provide companion for own child	4
To extend own family because raising a family is enjoyable	7
To fill a gap in own lives	5
To take on a challenge	4
A means of self-expression	6
Really enjoy being with children	11
Parent was fostered or in residential care as a a child and wants to help other children in that position	2
To help a child in need	14
Religious sense of duty	4

disappointments after placement, we concluded that parents' motives were extremely important – not in the sense that a particular motivation is inherently good or bad, but because there had to be some matching of what the child needed with what the parents had to give and might expect in return. Those who wanted a first or subsequent child to complete their families would gain most satisfaction from a child who they felt really fitted in and who was welcomed as part of the family by relatives, friends and the community. Those whose motives were altruistic needed to know at some stage that the homes they had offered to children in need were indeed helping those children and allowing them to make progress. When we asked some families why they had persevered when things looked bleak, their answers often reflected their original reasons for offering their homes. This was the case with one mother who, though she came to realize that the teenager living with them would never really be one of the family, persevered because she couldn't bear the thought of her going back to the children's home. She told us that the only time she nearly gave up was when she became convinced that she could not help her and might even be making her worse. Thus we gave some thought to assessing whether the motives and needs of the parents matched the needs of the children.

In the initial discussion between the local authority and the project workers the needs of the children were given precedence. However, we also noted that in the majority of cases the parents had picked out the children rather than had the children suggested to them. Placements where the parents picked out the children tended to be the most successful, but only if the interests of the children were given precedence or treated as equal in importance to the wishes and needs of the new families. When attention to the child's needs gave way to the pressure to find a child for a family who had been waiting for some time, the likelihood of success was much diminished. The following comments were made by social workers on this issue:

Several families were approved as adopters before the project started. We felt there was some obligation to place. Most of the introductions with pre-project families haven't worked out.

The more choice the family has the better chance of a real attachment being formed.

With some of the 'failed' introductions it was quite clear that important needs of the children were being ignored, and that the child in question would not be able to offer the prospective new parents what they were looking for. All except three of the 15 families got the type of child they had asked for. A social worker remarked of one mother, 'She got the daughter she'd always wanted. It couldn't have been better if the child had been born to her.'

Only one family had placed with them a child with the type of handicap they had specifically stated that they did not want. This was a childless couple who had asked for a young child with a physical handicap but had said they did not think they could cope with a mentally handicapped youngster. They were linked with a child who was physically handicapped but, as later became evident, was mentally handicapped as well. However, the parents themselves were not openly dissatisfied. The father said, 'I took a liking to him when I first saw him. I thought the doctors overstated his handicap. They looked on the glummest side. He's better than we expected.' By the two-year stage they had grown to love him, and were beginning to accept that his intellectual potential was likely to be more limited than they had at first hoped.

When the children talked about their own needs and wishes, they tended to think in concrete terms, such as whether or not the new family should have any children of their own and how old they should be, or what pets they should have. An 11-year-old mentally handicapped youngster wanted a family who would 'live in a town . . . have a bungalow . . . and a new car'. He also wanted his new family to be young. The family eventually chosen for him after a two-year search was different in every respect. When first interviewed he complained about this discrepancy, but as the placement proceeded he appeared to grow fond of his new parents despite the contrast between reality and the family of his dreams.

The matching of the parents' motivation with the child's needs was also important because motivation affected the way in which the family tried to help the child settle into their home, and how they coped with difficulties and differences. Most families set out from an early stage consciously to 'claim' the children as their own. Whilst they were willing to accommodate a child's differences in the short term and adapt their family lives accordingly, most, and especially those whose motivation inclined towards self-interest and whose aim was adoption, were clear that the child would sooner or later have to take on their preferred pattern of family life.

Ways of claiming the child varied with age. Names were important symbols of belonging and even some of the older children were surprisingly quick to take on the surname of the new family. This was mostly in order to satisfy a desperate need to be 'normal', but also because they had sensed that this would please their parents. In two cases school-age children decided to change their Christian names. Deciding when to start calling new paretns 'mum' and 'dad' was also important. Parents and social workers carefully prepared the ground for name changes, and children who were finding it difficult to make the change asked for help. Martin, aged nine, asked, 'When are we going to start the "mum and dad"? Can we start now?' One family enthusiastically joined in their new son's game of 'trying on' different Christian names to see how they fitted, and other families used role play with children. One family with a school-aged child used games to help her get into the swing of their family's way of doing things, and she entered into the spirit of this with great enthusiasm, being quite unused to this amount of attention. Most parents very deliberately reinforced the new roles by referring to their spouse as 'mum' or 'dad', even though the child might be at the stage of using their

Christian names. Other families, especially if there was continued parental contact, were more relaxed about things. One father observed, 'Having been fostered myself, I know you can't call two people mum. I think we will leave it and see what comes from them.'

Motivation also made a difference to the 'coping strategies' of the new parents – how they handled problem behaviour at the later stages of placement and, indeed, the extent to which they would tolerate difficult or different behaviour. Those who wanted the child to be very much part of their family, doing things the way their family did things, were more inclined to be explicit about the sort of behaviour which was required of a family member. Following a brush with the police about 18 months after placement, the parents of one teenage boy had a discussion with him about what he must do if he wanted to stay there. This was not done, as it sometimes is, in a spirit of threat – 'You behave, or out you go' – but rather in the spirit of imparting information: 'If you cannot make yourself a part of this family, things will get so difficult that it will not work out, or else the courts will intervene and remove you.' One father remarked, 'If you take a child in, and he's going to be there for life, you've got to start somewhere and tell them what you don't like.' We did wonder if the lad himself would appreciate the difference, but in our interviews with him he seemed to understand and appreciate this direct approach. Having experienced three breakdowns of 'permanent' placements already, he was constantly preoccupied with how to make himself acceptable to this particular family, with whom he very much wanted to stay. Speaking of her new daughter, another mother said, 'She knows in no way would I send her away. But if she gets too much out of hand, I've explained to her she would have to go.'

This is not to imply that such families did not go to great lengths to help the children to adjust, and to cope with difficult behaviour whilst at the same time attempting to change it. One father reported, 'When things are bad we says, "Well she could have been worse. You get those that shoplift." Since she took those things, we've changed the shoplifting bit to something else.'

Parents whose prime motivation was altruism were more able to tolerate difference, and to accept that a child might never be fully integrated into their family. As one mother said,

I felt from the word go, you have to give them a chance. For all the things we have said about them, they are lovely little characters. They are affectionate and appreciative. I like the boys but I can't say they are like my own. You *have* to give them a chance. They would just end up in another home and get taken off the books as a bad job. Time is running out for them. However bad they were, we would find it hard not to soldier on.

The degree of disruption to their own children which parents were prepared to tolerate also depended on their reason for offering a home to a new child. The one breakdown occurred in a family where the parents had wanted a companion for their own child, although they also wanted to help a child in need. When their own child came in for bullying from his would-be companion, they decided that he could no longer stay with them. Other families, and especially those with a strong altruistic drive, were prepared to allow the needs of the newcomer to override the needs of their own children at least during the settling-in period and at times of stress. In the early stages of the placement of two older brothers, one of whom was very much an extravert and quickly made himself at home, one rather shy younger son of the family became so distressed at the competition for his parents' attention that he became withdrawn and began to pull his hair out. His family responded by giving him more attention but making it clear that his new brothers were there to stay and that he would have to learn to live with them, which over time he seemed to do. Another family seemed to take in their stride the attempt (apparently in a game) to hang an amiable and compliant but not very bright older adopted son. An older daughter objected strongly when her parents applied to adopt a handicapped younger boy. She told us she liked him a lot and wouldn't like him to leave, but her resentment that he had his own bedroom when she had been longing for a bedroom of her own and still hadn't got one had boiled over when the question of adoption came up. Her mother told us,

When she says she doesn't want him to be adopted, she will have to lump it if she doesn't like it. I'm not hurt. I respect her for being honest. She won't changed. She takes after me. I'm using my judgement as to how she will feel when it's all over. She isn't old enough to decide the fors and against.'

Where families did not have the reward of knowning that the children they had taken were beginning to be really part of their family, we discussed with them what it was that made them carry

on at considerable expense (emotional and financial) to themselves and their own children and sometimes to their relationships
with their neighbours or extended families. Essentially, they
needed to see some progress which could convince them that their
efforts had been worthwhile. However, we saw signs in some cases
that the determination not to give in was so strong that they would
find cause for optimism in the slightest indication of improvement.
One mother reported,

We got to the stage [at about 18 months after placement] of thinking we
couldn't help her. You gave her everything you could, it didn't seem to
help. We thought, what's going to happen to her if we send her back. That
would be it. At least we could go on trying, we might get somewhere.
Even after two years, I asked her if she was happy, if she wanted to go
back. She said, 'I don't mind.' I said, 'All right, when your social worker
comes, *you* can say something. I won't.' But she didn't.

Altruism was especially necessary if there had been an element
of self-interest which had not been fully satisfied. A father who
had wanted a daughter told us, 'I wish she'd talk more, so that I
could get closer to her. That hurt me, because I wanted to give her
so much.'

If the children could show they wanted to be there, this would
carry their parents through the most difficult behaviour. One
family had lost most of their friends, their business had suffered and
their grown-up children thought twice before visiting. The father
confessed, 'They are like a couple of guard dogs around here.
People tend to stay clear of us.' However, his wife said,

I've not got to the stage of sending them back. I've got to the stage when I
couldn't stand another hour – couldn't bear the thought of next week – but
not send them back. I don't think I could ever do it. I know, even if I *am*
tearing my hair out, they are as happy as sandboys.

In one or two cases where signs of success were few and far
between, the will to carry on had to be strengthened from outside
by social workers or neighbours telling the parents that they really
were doing a valuable job, and at times we could only put their
persistence down to religious or humanitarian considerations,
which brought their own spiritual rewards. In some cases where
siblings were placed together, we felt that there were times when
one sibling going through a bad patch owed his continued presence
in the home to the fact that a brother or sister was becoming well

attached and the parents wouldn't hurt that one by rejecting the other. One father took comfort from the fact that 'There is usually one being reasonable if the others are not.'

To summarize, in our opinion successful matching of needs and motivations was an important factor contributing to the high success rate of these placements. Most of the parents got the sort of child they wanted and whom they could help. Most of the children got the sort of family with whom they could feel as comfortable as their at times daunting problems would allow them to be.

LEVELS OF SATISFACTION WITH THE PLACEMENTS AFTER TWO YEARS

In 15 of the 21 placements, all members of the new families were very satisfied or satisfied with the placement. An adoptive father said of his new daughter, a Down's syndrome child, 'She's brought us a great deal of happiness', while a foster mother stated of her new 14-year-old son, 'He's just like one of the family . . . he's a pleasure to have around.'

Whether the children looked like other members of their new family and whether they were similar in personality to their new brothers and sisters often made an important contribution to satisfaction with the placement – perhaps more so than matching of child and family in terms of social class and material standards. Sense of humour was mentioned by several families as either a problem, because it was so different, or as helping the attachment process, because it was similar. 12 of the children had a physical resemblance to members of their new families. This was especially important for the children, who enjoyed being told this, and for childless couples who wanted their children to look as they might have done had they been born to them. A 14-year-old girl told us that 'people often say I look like mum.' It was also noticed that mother and daughter dressed similarly and had their hair cut in similar styles.

For eight of the 15 families, the behaviour of one or more children made the adjustment period difficult, and, for four, jealousy from their own children or from husband or wife was an obstacle to their settling down together as a family. The mother of a seven-year-old boy who had come from a background which was culturally very different from that of his adoptive family was particularly upset by his insensitivity towards cherished family values such as kindness to pets. Once when he was caught ill-treating the dog she 'almost hit him' and 'found [herself] thinking about sending him back'. This was a case where in the early stages heart and head adjusted at different paces. Rationally the parents could understand and accept his behaviour. Emotionally, it was more difficult, but by the two-year stage, and especially after he was adopted, he seemed to be an important and secure member of the family. The lad whose first placement was disrupted was described as very disturbed. However, from his progress when placed in another family it became clear that the deterioration in his behaviour in the previous placement had not, as the social worker and family had assumed, been due to personality and behaviour difficulties which had not been made known to the family. Rather it seemed that this had just been the wrong home. The child had become unhappy, sensed that he was going to be rejected, and made sure he got in first with his rejection. A year after a teenager girl was placed with a couple who already had a teenage adopted son, the parents separated and the adopted son and father both turned against the foster child, blaming her for many of the problems. The foster mother, however, denied that the child had had anything to do with the family splitting up. She felt this had been 'inevitable' and that her husband and son were 'using Jean as a scapegoat'. Two years later the youngster had been adopted by her new mother, who had now married again.

Whether or not new families had their own children was important to the placement in 12 cases. Natural children helped to make some placements successful and threatened the stability of others, but most families were clear that having their own children made it easier to 'look after someone else's children', particularly if they had experience of a handicapped child. A mother with a Down's syndrome child of her own who adopted a baby with Down's syndrome said, 'We'd had it all before with our own daughter . . . we knew what to expect. . . . It's given us a new lease of life. We've been given a second chance, if you like.'

Although some felt their own children might have lost out, we were more often told that the arrival of a new brother or sister had been beneficial. Referring to her new sister a teenager daughter said, 'I think we are a much better family for having her. I'm more thoughtful for other people.' In particular, taking new children sometimes helped parents to see that they should allow their own children to grow up, and some conceded that they might have been over-protecting them before the new children arrived. The 'new lease of life' which some parents spoke of was perhaps a new and welcome lease of independence for one or more of their children.

In eight cases there were problems in relationships between the child and one or more new family members, and in seven of these cases this was owing to behaviour problems. The following examples were given by two mothers:

Mary wanted our son to be her boyfriend. How could we persuade her that he was her brother and not her boyfriend? I had to start talking to her about being in love.

Our own lad said, 'Mum if you don't get him out of my way I'll kill him!' He kept cheeking him in front of his friends. I say to my own, 'If they are hanging around you yoo much, tell them nicely.'

A 15-year-old girl caused her foster mother a great deal of anguish by her stealing and deceit, and this badly affected their relationship. The mother commented, 'There have been times when we thought we couldn't help her – she tries to hurt me – it got to the stage when we were uncomfortable in the house with her around. . . .' Jenny herself was reasonably satisfied with the placement even though she saw herself as the 'odd one out' in the family, in part because she was the only girl. She told us, 'I don't get treated like the rest. . . . I'm expected to do more in the house. . . . It's OK here. . . .'

A 15-year-old boy annoyed his foster sisters by his unacceptable behaviour and this caused friction. His foster father added, 'Mandy tells him how foul he is. . . . Jane is always fighting with him. . . .' In another case, the relationship between a 14-year-old boy and his foster mother and father broke down at one stage because of the boy's anti-social behaviour. The foster mother said, 'We felt as if we wanted to send him back. . . . he'd go berserk and I felt very frightened . . . he bruised Jack's arm and he had to have it strapped up.'

We asked the parents if they considered that their marriage had suffered in any way as a result of the placement, and if the child had attempted to come between them or caused trouble between them. Several parents said they had worried at some stage that their husband or wife might get hurt, either because the child was taking longer to become attached to that parent or because their partner would be very upset if the placement did not succeed.

Occasionally parents mentioned more frequent arguments as a result of differences of opinion about how to treat the child, and occasionally the increased stress and tiredness led to a worsening of the marriage for a while:

She needed so much of my time. I devoted hours of time. It's paid off. But my son and husband thought it wasn't necessary. Sometimes I didn't always feel like it but she needed it. I could guarantee she would be stuck as close as could be. My husband thought it wasn't necessary. (Mother)

She kept hanging round me all the time, I kept thinking of ways of putting her off without hurting her. I just couldn't hurt her. I never imagined my wife could be jealous. We'd been together for 17 years and she had never been jealous. (Father)

However, in the long run, only the father whose marriage broke up considered that the marriage had suffered, and several said that the arrival of the newcomer had improved their marriage:

I get a bit tired. But it gives you an interest. We've had our problems, with my husband's ill health. So we have got down. We have got an interest now. (Mother)

We've got more to talk about these days. (Father)

SUMMARY

In planning this research, one of our aims was to identify any patterns in the emotional development of the new families which it might be helpful for families and social workers involved in permanent placement of older and handicapped children to bear in mind. We found that the process for the babies and toddlers was different from that for the older children, with the younger school-age children falling into one camp or the other. The new families of the younger children made steady progress towards becoming attached, even though they progressed at different speeds. Adoption was an important stage for all of them, but in most cases not essential to the attachment process. The father of a Down's toddler affirmed, 'Adoption didn't make a scrap of difference. She was ours from when we first saw her.'

For some of the parents it was 'love at first sight'. For others, one parent felt drawn to the child and had an anxious time until the feelings of the other parent or their other children caught up. When the child finally arrived, there was sometimes a period of 'post-placement blues', partly brought on by tiredness and, especially where the child was handicapped, not helped by the number of well-meaning visitors (ourselves included), most offering advice which the family could not absorb all at once and perceived as there partly to check on them. There was also the problem of what the neighbours and extended family said. Sometimes they were full of praise and offers of help. Sometimes they made snide remarks about 'only doing it for the money' or the damage the parents would do to their own children. After a few months all the families who had taken younger children had made steady progress towards attachment and had begun to work on how they were going to help the children overcome any handicaps and how to tell them about adoption. What, for instance, would the reaction of a Down's child be, and how would she understand it? They went about their caring tasks with thought and energy, and, after love, energy was in most cases the quality which they most needed. Their main complaint was not difficult behaviour but their own tiredness, a problem not to be underestimated, as most were older than the normal age for romping on the floor with toddlers.

The process for the older children was more complex. Sometimes it was 'love at first sight' for parent or child, but more often attraction grew more slowly and at different rates for different members of the family. As with the younger children, there was sometimes a 'low' period after the excitement of introductions and the final move. Fortunately, for all except two of the families, this coincided with the child's 'honeymoon' period. Overtly disturbed behaviour did not usually start straightaway, but the 'differentness' of the children could not be avoided when they were there day in, day out, and strategies had to be worked out for coping. Cover stories had to be agreed on and stuck to by all members of the family. One family decided they preferred the term 'step-sister' to 'foster sister'. Others used 'adopted sister', even if adoption was not envisaged. Some children had to learn that arguments between husband and wife were normal and did not threaten the placement. One mother noted, 'We had to be careful at first if we had arguments. He said, "What would happen if you divorced, would I get sent back?" '

Not only did most of the children go through a 'honeymoon' period, but several made a point of telling their new families how pleased they were to be there and how much they loved them. One mother reported of an eight-year-old, 'At about three months he said, "I've fallen in love with you and dad. When I'm at work, I'll still live here." ' A teenage girl left notes around the house telling her mother she loved her. Only one mentally handicapped teenage lad repeatedly told his new parents that he wanted to go back to the children's home, although others sometimes flung this out in anger.

We felt that 'being in love' rather than 'loving' was the appropriate description of the children' feelings at this stage, but such expression of affection helped the families over their own awkward stage. We considered that the parents became attached to the children more quickly than the children to them. For all the older children, this 'in love' stage had to give way to a testing-out period before a more trusting relationship could grow, and even by two years after placement some of the children had not yet reached this point. Sometimes there was a prolonged period of difficult behaviour. More often it came in spells, or else good behaviour most of the time would be broken sometimes by an outburst which rocked the family because they had been feeling good about how well things were going. By the two-year stage, each family in our study had found a way of living together, a kind of loving, which was more rewarding to some than to others, but of no family did we feel that no ties of affection existed.

8

The Process of Child Placement

The planning meetings were excellent. No one was patron-
izing. Nobody was wanting to take a more important role.
Everyone was working for the good of the children.

(Local authority social worker)

Joint working is a matter of trust. Whether they can trust you
to do the work properly with the family. Trust your
judgement. The local authority panel had to approve the
linking. I was made to feel we were all a bunch of amateurs. I
was going to be told what to do. There was no trust in my
ability.

(Project social worker)

THE LOCAL AUTHORITY SOCIAL WORKERS

In this chapter we consider the complex system for linking
voluntary and statutory agencies, sometimes at opposite ends of
the country, and sometimes involving five different field or
residential social workers for one case. Brief details of the project
social workers have already been given, in chapter 3, and, since
good professional relationships and mutual respect are essential to
any successful co-operative enterprise, we start by considering the
professional backgrounds of the local authority social workers
referring the children.

22 workers were involved with the 29 study children. All except
one (from a Scottish authority) were interviewed, and in that case
a questionnaire was completed. There was 18 women and four
men; three were aged under 30, and three were over 50. Only four
were not qualified, and only two had less than two years'

experience. Ten had been the child's social worker for six years or longer. Thus, although slightly younger on average than the project workers, the referring workers did not fit the 'young and inexperienced' label often used. All except three considered themselves to be specializing in child care work. The general impression from our interviews was of a group of skilled social workers, deeply concerned about the children they were seeking to place and prepared to make considerable efforts on their behalf.

From these details it would seem that there should have been sufficient common ground between the referring workers and project workers for them to be able to work well together and for the relationship to be based on professionalism and mutual respect. In the opinion of one local authority worker, 'They [the project workers] are doing a good job, and they have the freedom to be able to do it and the time. They are specialist resource finders, with the opportunities to do the sort of work we would like to do.'

However, although a common background and shared skills can help trust to develop, there was also the possibility of resentment or envy creeping into the feelings of busy local authority workers about their agency counterparts. All four project workers had been social services department employees and had brought with them ambivalent feelings about local authority work, especially its bureaucratic aspects. There was a tendency for project workers to undervalue local authority workers, usually in general but some-times in particular. More noticeable was the tendency to be critical of social services departments. The project workers may have felt some resentment that, especially with indirect referrals, the power at the decision-making stage was very much with the local authority, as personified by its social worker and home-finding panel, who had to decide whether a family approved by the project should be accepted or rejected.

THE REFERRAL PROCESS

Although detailed information was collected only on the 29 children in the case study group, questionnaires were used to collect basic information on all other children referred directly or linked indirectly with project families during the first three years. Over this period, 28 children were referred directly for placement by the project and there were 37 indirect referrals.

The direct referrals were made by seven local authorities and two voluntary agencies. The children referred indirectly were in the care of 15 local authorities and represented 23 family referrals. Referring authorities included seven counties, a large city and seven London boroughs, ranging as far afield as south London, the West Midlands and Scotland. This spread of referrals allowed us to build up a fairly extensive picture of child care policy and practice. From our interviews, we were able to divide referring departments rather crudely into those whose policy was that links with natural families should if possible be maintained, and who in consequence were more likely to seek 'secure' foster placements (two authorities); those who saw permanence as the major goal but had no strong preference for adoption or secure fostering as the means of achieving this (two authorities); and those who saw adoption as the aim for all but a small minority of (probably older) children (six authorities). We had insufficient information to decide about the other five. We found these different perceptions of the best way to achieve permanence to have an important bearing on inter-agency co-operation and the establishment of trust between project and local authority workers. From our analysis of referring authorities it seems that those seeing long-term fostering as a valid route to permanence were under-represented. Such authorities are likely to use the *Foster Care* newsletter or newspaper advertising rather than the BAAF or PPIAS as a source of recruitment for substitute families.

We now consider the referral process in more detail as it concerned the 48 children on whom we have basic information (the 29 children in the main study, together with 19 children referred later, whose social workers completed questionnaires; this is a 75 per cent sample of the 64 children referred in the first three years). We found that the 19 children referred later shared the characteristics of the study children as described in chapter 4.

As mentioned in chapters 1 and 4, adoption policy has changed recently not only because of the inclusion of older and handicapped children amongst those for whom adoption is considered appropriate, but also because of the placing for adoption of growing numbers of children whose parents do not request it and who often oppose it. For this reason we pause here to consider in more detail the referral process as it affects children who are considered to need secure placements, but who are still in touch with members of their natural families. As anticipated, we did meet a wide range of views about how to proceed in such cases. Some workers considered that the only way to achieve permanence was to sever ties and then place for adoption, even if this meant moving a child who was well settled in a long-term foster home; others felt that a permanent placement would only be acceptable if the child could remain in contact with significant people from the past. In between were those, the majority, who saw need for continued contact with members of the natural family as one aspect to be considered alongisde others. If no family able to meet all identified needs was available, then other needs, perhaps for special help with a handicap, might be regarded as taking precedence over the need for continued parental contact. Again, whereas some workers saw the *status of adoption* as being the main way to achieve permanence but were willing to be flexible about the need for contact, others felt most strongly that, whatever the legal status, permanence might well be jeopardized if contact were not terminated before a child was introduced to a new family. Some were for decisive action to terminate contact, place for adoption and apply for dispensation with parental consent; others inclined towards a more gradual approach and were more likely to ask for a secure foster placement where parental contact could continue, so long as it was of value to the child and did not jeopardize the placement. The following two contrasting referrals through the ARE illustrate the differing models of permanence requested.

Probably long-term fostering needed because of ongoing links with the natural family.

It would be a contested adoption, with the problem of sibling contact. There was sadness that they could not be with their real mum and dad and that their brother could not be with them, but also excitement and the hope of love and security.

Before a referral could be made, skilled and time-consuming work was needed with the natural family, the caretakers and the child, in order to assess their wishes and feelings, and to come to a conclusion about how the child's welfare 'throughout his childhood' could best be safeguarded. In three cases in our study, problems resulted because children were referred too quickly by enthusiastic workers who had heeded the message that children should not be allowed to wait too long in care. A senior worker whose home-finding committee had agreed to a referral to the ARE was able to say, with the benefit of hindsight,

The work hadn't been properly done either with the child or the parents. The natural family was not ready, therefore it should not have been a placement for adoption. If a local authority takes action which makes it impossible for parents to see a child without having worked out why it is doing it, it gives two messages – you can see your child, but you have a day's journey to do so. We want to get earlier decisions, but you have got to play fair by all sides. The child and the parents went along with the view that this would be a traditional long-term family. The resentment on all sides showed through later on.

In most agencies there was a managerial split between long-term fostering and adoption, it being assumed that long-term foster placements would be made at area team level. Any departure from this had to be strongly argued for, partly because of cost: it is one thing to argue for spending £3,000 if the child will then be adopted and off the area's books, and another to argue for an outlay of £1,047 when boarding-out allowances will still need to be paid, plus a fee for the voluntary agency to continue to supervise after 12 months if the child is placed at some distance. Project workers resented the loss of fees where children who with hindsight were considered to have been inappropriately referred were withdrawn from the project – especially if a great deal of time had been spent with the child and potential new family. It was in part owing to such losses, where the project obtained no recompense for the use of its own resources, that later in the study period the agency was doing less work with children.

Money was also relevant at the referral stage in so far as it affected the type of permanent placement requested. In at least two cases, birth parents of older children were influenced in their decision to consent to adoption because of their liability to pay parental contributions for children so long as they remained in care. Pressure was put on one new family to proceed more quickly to adoption than they thought appropriate because the natural mother was being prosecuted for non-payment of parental contributions. This factor is particularly relevant if a parent (usually a father) has remarried and the requirement to pay contributions and the threat of prosecution cause problems for the new marriage and any children of that marriage.

We have been discussing the process of referral to specialist agencies in general, and will now move to a consideration of the reasons for referring to this particular agency. Social workers were asked what sort of children they would consider referring to the

CWAH and their reasons for referring a particular child. Table 8.1 summarizes their responses.

Most of the workers responsible for children referred indirectly said that they would refer all types of handicapped children if they

Table 8.1 Reasons given by social workers for referral to CWAH (direct referrals only – 16 families)

Reason	Number of times mentioned
The child needed to be placed at a distance	3
The proximity of the agency	3
The expertise of the project workers in finding and supporting families	11
The expertise of the project workers in preparing children for permanent placement	1
Social worker's lack of time to do the work properly	11
The child was especially difficult to place	7
Shared work and planning would mean that there would be a better chance of success	2
Because of previous failed attempts at finding a permanent home for this child, the worker had lost confidence in her own ability to do so and felt a need to bring in specialists	2
Had tried unsuccessfully to find a permanent placement	3
The project is prepared to take risks in approving the out-of-the-ordinary families which local authorities tend to turn down but which seem to succeed with 'hard-to-place' children	3
The children's home was closing and the agency did not have the resources to find permanent homes for several children at once	3
The project will make secure foster placements and encourage contact with members of the natural family	2

either needed to place at a distance, needed to place quickly (as with handicapped babies) and did not have a placement immediately available, or had tried on their own and failed to make a placement. Most said they would only refer for adoption and not for fostering. Typical answers were

I would like to refer for all sorts of placements but it is dictated by the employing agency's resources.

All sorts of permanent home. It's a flexible project. The needs of the child are considered and matched with the needs of the family.

RECRUITMENT OF POTENTIAL NEW FAMILIES

We consider this in more detail in chapters 6 and 9, but a few comments are appropriate here about the way in which inter-agency work affected recruitment. Table 8.1 shows that three local authority workers mentioned the voluntary agency's ability to be more adventurous, to 'take risks', in its recruitment policy as being one of the reasons for referring. Social workers who kept up to date with the literature on child placement were aware that often it was unconventional families who succeeded with 'special needs' children.

The willingness of the project workers to look beyond first or even second impressions and discover what a family had to offer was welcomed in theory by those referring children, but was also a source of tension, and possibly conflict, when it came to linking families and children. Experience of the more conventional families approved by local authorities, and the inclination to find a nice ordinary family for 'their' child, meant that social workers sometimes felt disappointment on meeting the proposed family. It was at such times that trust in the professionalism and skill of the project worker became crucial. One local authority worker commented,

That was the bit that really tested the co-operation – when I first met the family. On paper, I was over the moon. When I met them, they were not what I expected. But I told myself, it wasn't my role to do all the interviews again. But it does make you feel it's out of your control.

This placement was made and proved to be one of the happiest ones in our study. In a similar case a child was withdrawn from referral because the local authority worker, under pressure from the child's foster parents and natural family, decided that the linking was unsuitable: 'Had it been a conventional family, there would have been no resistance.' Another child was later successfully placed in that home.

PREPARATION OF THE CHILD AND WORK WITH
THE NATURAL FAMILY

The person mainly responsible for preparing the child was the local authority field or residential worker or the foster parent, except in three cases where the project worker had the principal role. With seven other children (from four families) the preparation work was shared between residential workers and project worker, and for six others (three families) joint work was undertaken by local authority field workers and project workers. For children referred directly, the planning meeting held shortly after referral allocated roles and reached tentative conclusions about the sort of home which might be needed. Comments about planning meetings were generally positive, but in a few cases tension surfaced about respective roles, power and control. Potential causes of tension were feelings about local authorities or voluntary agencies, attitudes about the best way to achieve permanence and the role to be played by natural parents, and views about the legal steps to be taken.

The project workers felt strongly that with direct referrals they should take over professional direction of the case, and where this was accepted by the referring agency there was unlikely to be conflict. The project workers' authority was increased by their expertise and their familiarity with the issues, especially when the local authority worker had not had any previous experience of placing a child through another agency. Jargon helped to augment this effect:

They seem to know quite what they want. A bit too much sometimes. I felt rather organized by them.

A by-product of their work is to educate others. At first I thought the jargon was a bit 'twee'. But they were always very willing to talk and explain.

Even when they were not the prime workers for the child, the project workers often advised the residential or field workers. Most workers – especially residential workers, who were often unused to being so fully involved – greatly appreciated this partnership. One residential worker commented, 'The planning meeting was very good. Everyone was in the picture. Everyone was part of what was going on. In the past, the emphasis would be on the field worker. The staff would be left out. This is a much better system.'

We received no negative comments from local authority workers about co-operation with project workers in preparing children for new families. However, in retrospect project workers were critical of some of the preparatory work, especially where children were withdrawn, and felt that it would have been better if they had been more involved.

An important part of the preparation stage is work with the natural parents. The main worker for the parents was invariably the local authority field worker, although the project worker might offer advice, or occasionally see the parents, particularly if the natural parents and new parents were to meet each other. Work with natural parents was more likely than work with children to be a source of friction with project workers, and in at least four cases disagreements arose, which were not always expressed at the time. To some extent, in offering a variety of secure placements, the project was at risk of giving mixed messages. It is clearly much easier for those referring to adoption agencies to know what is required of them before placement. These two comments about planning meetings serve to illustrate the point:

At the first planning meetings there were disagreements about the legal side. They [the local authority workers] wanted a permanent home but they hadn't faced up to terminating parental contact. We felt they had to terminate contact. They didn't agree. The conflict started there. (Project worker)

I like the specialist agencies because we all get together at a planning meeting. You can refer your complicated situations. You don't have to have it cut and dried before you refer. Then we all work together. Get support with the difficult decisions. They fire us with enthusiasm about the work that needs doing with children and families. (Local authority worker)

DECIDING ON THE NEEDS OF THE CHILD AND
LINKING CHILD AND NEW FAMILY

For direct referrals, the likely needs of the child were identified at the planning meeting, and for indirect referrals the social workers would also refine their views about the sort of home they were looking for when potential new families were suggested.

Local authority and project workers were asked to list, for each of the children, the characteristics they were looking for in a new family. Usually they were quite specific about whether they wanted children to be placed with siblings, and whether they wanted them to have contact with parents or siblings placed elsewhere, but otherwise they wanted to leave open as many options as possible. Although the majority of the children lived in towns or cities, the geographical environment was rarely mentioned as significant, and this was also the case with social class. Workers were more likely to talk in terms of personal characteristics, such as the child's need for a family who would not be too demanding. We then looked at each suggested linking to see if it fitted with what had been asked for. For 19 children (14 placed and five withdrawn) it did, whilst for ten (eight placed and two withdrawn) it did not.

Not surprisingly, the project workers thought that all proposed placements would meet all or most of the identified needs, but in eight cases the local authority workers had serious doubts, though believing that the placement was the best available and worth the risk. In one case, even though the placement proceeded, the local authority worker said he thought it was unlikely to meet the child's needs.

The stage at which the local authority worker met the suggested family for the first time was commonly agreed to be the major test of inter-agency co-operation, especially for those workers who had known the children for a long time and were likely to have some sort of ideal family in mind. Reservations were not always expressed at the time. In the course of the research interviews some local authority workers told us how relieved they were that they had had enough trust in the project worker's greater knowledge of the families to recommend that the placement go ahead. Others who had had their doubts regretted they had not expressed them at that stage and avoided letting a child down. For direct referrals this delicate stage was sometimes complicated by the fact that the project worker who was concerned with the child, and with whom the local authority had been liaising up to this point, was not the one working with the family. Sometimes both project workers were at this meeting, one to support the family and help them make a decision about whether this would be the right child for them, and one to look at it from the child's point of view.

There was some confusion about the exact purpose of the meeting between the local authority worker and proposed new family. The decision about linking has to be taken by the home-finding panel or case committee of the local authority, but all were agreed that the recommendation of the individual social worker was of great importance in swaying this meeting. However, the fact that a panel was ultimately responsible for the decision was welcome. Of one case a local authority worker remarked, 'It was such a difficult decision to move him from a foster home where he was well settled. I was grateful for the panel meeting.'

The presence of the project worker at the panel meeting was appreciated if the family was one unlikely to be approved by the local authority in the normal course of events. However, for the project worker this could be an uncomfortable meeting, not only because her professional pride could be ruffled by scrutiny of her work, but also because of protective and proprietorial feelings for the family being examined. One project worker complained, 'They seemed to think I wanted their boy for my lovely family. They were picking them to pieces.'

Prospective families did not go to panel meetings to put their own case, so the meeting with the child's social worker was an important and stressful one for them. This was particularly so if previous similar meetings had come to nothing. Although both parties would be hoping to get something out of the meeting – a child, or a home for a child – both were at the same time using the meeting to decide whether this was really what they wanted, and also to impress the other party in case they decided they *did* want to go ahead.

The prime purpose of this meeting was for the child's social worker to provide the family with as much information as they needed in order to make a decision about whether to proceed. All the local authority workers we interviewed acknowledge that at this stage they could not, and should not, undertake a second home study, but had to trust the project workers' assessment that the family were suitable for a child with special needs. However, it had to be decided whether they could meet the needs of the child in question. The family's project worker needed to be present in order to assist with her detailed knowledge of them, to ensure that all areas of possible difficulty with the child were explored, and to help the family to ask the right questions about the child. However, the two social workers were likely also to see themselves as advocates for, respectively, the child and the new family. By this stage in the proceedings, even families whose motives were strongly altruistic either very much wanted the child, or at least wanted to be offered the chance of saying no, and the project workers, especially if the family had been waiting some time, very much hoped the linking would be successful. A local authority worker commented, 'They are very involved with *their* families and they want to find children for *their* families.'

Taking into account all these very complex issues of need, power, self-esteem and professional prickliness, it is hardly surprising that these meetings were so stressful. It is our view that many later difficulties had their roots in this first meeting, but that doubts and anxieties were not fully expressed until later.

It was especially important that this meeting should not be allowed to commit anyone too far, so that all parties could have time to absorb information and think things over. A local authority worker told us,

That was the bit that really tested the co-operation. I felt I can't allow myself to have reservations. I haven't gone into it in the same depth as they have. They admitted they had had the same reservations in the past. I felt their worker [whom she hadn't met before] was very defensive about them. I was trying to say my concern is what the children will feel. There was a bit of ill-feeling. It was a great relief to go home and not to sit down and make a plan.

In another case, however, the local authority worker felt under pressure to commit himself further than he wished at that first meeting. On this occasion two project workers – one for the child and one for the family – were present. The local authority worker complained,

I felt ganged up on. The family was very keen. That's where the issue of who does what and whose decision it is comes up again. I felt quite confused. They were extremely nervous foster parents who thought I was coming to approve them. I had the feeling that the meeting went further than it should have done – of having no control over the situation. I said to my team leader that I had to let go of that bit, the approving bit. That is what we asked to agency to do. But I had the feeling that I had allowed it to go too fast.

We would suggest that ample time should be available, preferably with the two workers spending time together before meeting the family, to discuss respective roles during the meeting. There should also be time afterwards to discuss any areas of doubt or disagreement, and the project worker, being more familiar with the process, should help the local authority worker express uncertainities and try to resolve them. It was clear from our interviews that several workers felt inhibited about expressing their concerns to, or asking too many questions of, the project workers at this stage, as they did not wish to seem to be questioning their professional competence.

THE MEETING BETWEEN THE CHILD AND THE FAMILY

We were reminded, in discussing the progress of each case, of the making of a huge snowball. Started with a nucleus of parents and child, it rolled along picking up bits along the way in the form of residential workers, foster parents, local authority social workers and panels, the CWAH workers and panel, and sometimes losing bits (fathers, mothers, relatives, previous foster parents). By the time the child was introduced to a new family, the snowball seemed to have grown to rather large proportions, especially if no bits had been shed on the way, and, whilst not everyone was actually present at the first meeting between the child and the new family, their interests had to be represented, or they were referred to as presences in the background.

The introductory meetings between the child and the family were their opportunity to decide whether there was a reasonable chance that they could live together. Whatever had been put down on paper, the 'chemistry' had to be right, and the project workers put a great deal of effort into stage-managing the first meeting to make the event as relaxed as possible. 'Stage-managing' is an appropriate term, since by this point the possible 'cast' included the child, the natural parents and siblings, the previous caretakers, the present caretakers, specialist teachers or physiotherapists, the local authority social worker, the new parents, their own children, their important close relatives, the project worker for the child and the project worker for the family. How many should be involved in the first meeting? What was the right combination of participants? Obviously it was often advisable for a number of meetings to be arranged for the new parents to meet everybody it was thought they needed to, and sometimes the first meeting set in motion a whole round of visits.

At least the following would be present at the first meeting: the child or children to be placed, the new parents, the project worker for the family, and the local authority social worker or residential worker or foster parent. Most often the meeting took place on the child's home ground, but sometimes it was thought appropriate for a child, as one worker put it, 'to see the whole package straight away', so the meeting would be arranged in the home of the new family. The largest number present at an introduction was 11, and on this occasion a minibus was used to make a tour of the children's regular haunts. This was described by all concerned as most successful, with the greater part of a whole day being set aside for different participants in the process to spend time with each other and to unwind. With handicapped babies, social workers might take the new parents on a round of meetings with consultants, who could discuss with them a child's problems, prognosis and treatment, but otherwise would leave the prospective new parents with the child and foster parents to get to know each other in more initimate surroundings.

It would seem from the comments of families and children that the stage-managing paid off. Although these meetings were remembered as being nerve-racking events, this was recognized as inevitable; families' comments indicated excitement and pleasure mingled with sadness at the child's unhappy past or present and impatience to get things moving. Usually by this stage the linking would already have been approved in principle by the local authority and project panels, and the prospective parents would know that they and the child would now have a major part in the decision to proceed or not and would thus be less liable to frustration than at the matching stage.

If, following the first meeting, it was decided that the intro-duction should proceed, a planning meeting would be held involving the new family, sometimes the foster parents, the two agencies, and any other significant professionals, such as resi-dential workers, teachers or therapists. The purpose of this meeting would be to decide how to proceed with introductions, to agree on the payment of fees and the level of boarding-out and other allowances, and to decide whether the child should be placed immediately for adoption or should be placed initially as a foster child under boarding-out regulations. Decisions were also made about legal action to be taken and about the respective roles of the workers with the child, the natural family, the caretakers and the new family. For indirect referrals this was the first encounter of the local authority worker with other members of the project staff and their methods of working, and comments tended to be favourable. Again, the 'training' role of the project workers was appreciated.

This was the time when the new parents, having met the children, learned more about them and in the light of that knowledge could decide whether to go ahead. Only one family in the study dropped out at this stage. We asked the parents if with hindsight they thought they had been given a fair picture of the children. Most of the 14 families of the successfully placed children said they had, but then usually added a rider that it was difficult for social workers to know how a child would be in *their* home. It should be noted here that it was not common practice for the family's project worker to meet the child before deciding whether a linking should proceed. There may well have been some value in such a meeting in the case of older children, as a worker knowing the family well might have picked out aspects of a youngster's personality or behaviour significant to the new family. Thus, a very quiet family commented that they were not told how noisy and aggressive the child was, and this was a major source of concern for them. To another family his behaviour might have been seen as high spirits, and only a social worker who knew the family well would have been likely to visualize the child in their home and feel this aspect of his personality deserved comment. Social workers tend to list known behaviour difficulties such as bed-wetting, but it is difficult to know which features of a child's personality might cause annoyance to a particular family.

It is not easy to say whether more could have been done to make the families really aware of the sort of child they were to take into their home *before* introductions were well under way and it was possible to draw back without harm being done. The difficult dynamics of the meeting at which the social worker talks about the child have been discussed, and are such that it is doubtful if the family takes in all that is said and highly likely that they listen selectively. One family's project worker commented, 'On a rational level they had accepted the idea of an older child. They had waited for so long. They had had one let-down. She [the prospective mother] was too bubbly and enthusiastic. She wasn't listening.'

Clear written information is essential, but we concluded that parents who felt inadequately prepared had in mind not what children *did* but what they *were* – their personality rather than their behaviour, and it is not easy to put personality down on paper. Most of the families said that the posters which the children made for publicity purposes were shallow and unhelpful and that television appearances created too rosy a picture. When things did not work out too well, the obvious scapegoat was the local authority social worker, who was seen as having failed to pass on vital information, but we came to the unhelpful conclusion that, if the 'chemistry' was not right, angelic behaviour would not rescue the situation and behaviour difficulties not revealed by social workers were handy face-savers. One parent who decided against proceeding after having been introduced to a child said, 'He was too good to be true. But I felt exasperated most of the time. A younger child would have been easier to love. How do you warm to a fourteen year old lad?'

THE INTRODUCTORY PERIOD

If the meeting between a child and potential new family was a stage during which inter-agency relationships tended to go well, the next stage was likely to put them to the test. As one adoptions officer put it, 'We have no problems at the referral stage from our own social workers. We are used to referring to specialists. It's when at the planning meeting the key worker role is given to specialists that problems occur.' If cracks have been previously papered over, it is at this stage that they are likely to reappear, as in one case where the project worker said, 'There was a slight difference of perception about the child's need, but she [the local authority worker], soon caved in'. In another case the local authority worker said of the first meeting with a family which withdrew after a youngster had been introduced, 'I had a gut feeling of unease which I didn't express. I persuaded myself that there were enough positives to go ahead.'

Although local authority field and residential workers would be likely to continue to play important roles with the children in the early stages of an introduction, to assess how it was going, the project workers jealously guarded their 'prime worker' status with the new families. If a local authority worker knew the child well, as was often the case, and particularly if he was not based too far away or had contact because of helping with transport, it was very hard for him not to discuss the family's reactions. One such worker commented,

I felt I had a lot of information. But I wasn't the one working with the family. I wasn't able to say, well that's because . . . I certainly found that difficult. It is one of the drawbacks. There would be a lot to be said for the social worker for the child going in independently and getting to know them in the context of the child.

Project workers varied as to how strongly they felt about any involvement of the local authority worker with the family. One felt it was a distinct advantage if the local aurhority worker had not known the child very long, because then he would be prepared to hand over to the project. Another preferred to work closely with a child's worker, and would sometimes ask her to visit for a particular purpose. One said, 'If they have a good worker they know well, there is safety there. I try not to get too close to the child because they need to attach to a new family.'

This stance of slightly distance concern was appreciated by those local authority workers who realized that someone who was less involved might have a role to play with the child. As one remarked, 'Because I have known Jean for so long, there are a lot of feelings involved. She is good at protecting adults, not wanting to hurt me. I found it easier to know there was someone outside who would allow her to say what she wanted to say.'

The other issue likely to cause conflict during the introductory period, if it had not been resolved earlier, was that of continued contact with members of the natural family. At this stage the new parents and children were liable to 'play out' the previous disagreements between workers about the sort of placement needed. A child staying the weekend with his potential new mum and dad, and whose contact with his mother had been temporarily terminated to allow him to form new attachments, put up her photo in what was to be his bedroom. The prospective parents, a childless couple really wanting a baby of their own, found this too difficult to cope with and decided they could not go on with the placement. If the social worker's message that he really needed placement with continued contact with members of his birth family had been heeded at the planning stage, it is highly unlikely that this 'match' would have got as far as this. In another case, a child whose contact had been officially terminated was, without telling anyone, going to see his parents during the introduction to his new family. That introduction also failed, and anger was directed against the local authority worker for not knowing about these 'secret' visits.

There was little disagreement between workers about the length of introductions. The details were agreed at the planning meeting with the new parents, but, despite this, and despite the fact that most introductions were comparatively short, most new families found them too long and stressful and put pressure on the workers to let things happen more quickly. As the introductions proceeded, the new parents and the children became major forces in their own right in the decision-making process. To return to our snowball analogy, bits of the large ball in evidence at the time of the first meeting would, if all went well, break off or shrink in significance to leave a nucleus of the new parents, the child and the project worker, with the local authority social worker and sometimes members of the natural family more or less firmly attached to the edge. The final decision to proceed was taken at a reconvened planning meeting, but the families and children themselves, now that they had a major say, assumed that placement would go ahead unless either of them decided otherwise. The final planning meeting was an important safeguard, and a useful time for deciding about practical, financial and social work support. However, where introductions did not proceed to placement the decisions were taken earlier, usually unilaterally, by child, project worker or new family. Only one child who was actually placed was removed during the period of our study, and our interviews with the social workers, the residential workers, the child and the family revealed nothing which, even with benefit of hindsight, should have warned the planning meeting that the placement should not have gone ahead.

THE DECISION NOT TO GO AHEAD

The potential for disagreement is obviously greater when things do not work out as anticipated, but in only two cases where introductions had eventually proved unsuccessful was any serious disagreement expressed by either worker, largely because by this stage most local authority workers had eased out of the situation and were content to let the project workers make the decisions. It is likely that conflict at this stage was related to what had happened in the past. Where a relationship of mutual trust existed, the workers were likely to share their sadness for child and family and work together on the next step. One worker was surprised when an introduction was terminated by a project worker without any warning or consultation, and another thought that perhaps if more effort had been made it could have succeeded, as relationships seemed to be basically good despite a particularly difficult incident. However, both had accepted that the project worker was the expert, and as the key worker her decision should be supported. This was also the view of the local authority social worker of the child who was withdrawn after placement, who commented that she would have been willing to visit twice a week if necessary, but that the project workers were on the spot and were the best judges of what was needed. She sent the child postcards so that he knew that she was aware of what was happening and was still concerned about him.

In one case the project worker and the family got rid of their anger and comforted each other by blaming the local authority worker for not knowing the child well enough and therefore not giving them enough information on which to base a decision. In two cases the anger was directed at the other social worker or her agency. The local authority worker in one of these cases complained,

I felt bitter. It made me feel sick to think of it. I had mixed feelings of wanting to dismember her, and feeling sorry for her. The introduction shouldn't have gone ahead. But I remember thinking, she has done the work with this couple. She is another professional, I have to take her word for it. It has made me quite sceptical about so-called expert agencies.

For indirect referrals, the failure of an introduction meant that there would be no further contact, other than to decide whether the child should return or keep the family's photo album given as part of the introductory process and to recover any possessions left at the last visit. In such cases, the anger (for it would seem that anger is almost inevitable) was directed at the child for not really wanting a new mum and dad in the first place, or at the family for 'not knowing their own minds'.

With children referred directly, a decision had to be made about whether another placement should be tried. One child was placed quickly, after a short period in a children's home, with another family who had previously expressed an interest in him. In another case, a family was interested in the child, but his father, on hearing that the first introduction had broken down, asked to be given a fresh chance of making a home for him. The local authority worker felt that this should at least be considered fully before looking at a new family, but there was considerable anger from the project workers as a result of this decision, perhaps reflecting the fact that throughout this case there had been concealed disagreement, so that by this stage the workers were not able to share their concerns openly. The local authority worker told us, 'Perhaps I hadn't involved them enough in what was happening. But they wouldn't accept what I wanted to do. I found it very painful. The conflict. The things that were being said.'

The importance of holding 'disruption meetings' has been stressed (Fitzgerald, 1983). In so far as they can help the people concerned to understand what went wrong and can stop the search for scapegoats, they are likely to be helpful. They may, with benefit of hindishgt, be able to spot mistakes and help with future plans for the child. In looking at the introductions in our sample which failed, we were able to spot possible explanations. But often there was at least one other case where in the same circumstances a new family seemed to be coping successfully.

POST-PLACEMENT SUPERVISION

Once the child had been placed, there was little room for argument about the respective roles of the social workers. Some local authority workers continued for a short period to visit the new families in their professional capacity, but this was welcomed in only one case. In the other cases, after one or two visits and sometimes none at all if the placement was for adoption, the local authority worker only visited for statutory reviews. There was contact with the authority over finance and equipment, and this was sometimes a cause of friction. Sometimes project workers accused authorities of meanness and unnecessary delay. Some local authority workers accused the project workers of colluding with the families and not accepting the full implications of the authority's legal responsibility for children in care, whilst wanting to get as much material help from the department as possible. At this stage the tendency for families to see the local authority worker as wholly bad, and the project worker as wholly good, was marked. We noted that families who at earlier interviews had spoken well of a local authority worker were now remembering only bad things.

Two important details about inter-agency work in the post-placement period should be mentioned here. The project workers saw their principal task at this stage as helping the new family to feel and behave like a family. Thus, they deliberately did not spend much time alone with the child and played down their official role. They did, however, sometimes have difficulty persuading local authority workers that it was inappropriate for them to spend time alone with the children. In this the project workers were arguing against what would normally be regarded as 'good practice' (DHSS, 1976, 1982) and might be seen as acting contrary to the spirit if not the letter of the Boarding-Out Regulations. However, this concept of good practice does not, in our view, sufficiently differentiate between the service appropriate to children placed for temporary periods, where the Regulations provide essential safeguards, and the service which is appropriate to children placed with foster parents who intend, and are intended, to be permanent substitute parents.

INTER-AGENCY CO-OPERATION: SUCCESS OR FAILURE?

We have considered the cost in financial terms. To conclude this chapter we refer to the human cost and to the issues of risk and anger, words which kept coming up in our interviews. Where there was a comparatively new local authority worker, or the project worker did not relate closely to the family or the child, then, when things did not work out as hoped, the workers would take it in their stride and move to make new plans and console those who had been hurt. But, for several of the children, it was the deep concern of the workers built up over the years which made them persist in looking for a new home, often after more than one failure and often against strong opposition. The decision to persist was usually a difficult one, rarely with a bouquet at the end, and with so many people to please that someone was likely to be hurt and angry. We found it unfortunate that some of those involved had difficulty coping with uncertainty and seemed to need to find a precise reason and a person to blame when plans did not work out. That person was usually the one who could most easily be isolated, as the following comments suggest.

Everyone was angry with the local authority social worker for different reasons. Towards the end of the introduction, I got seduced into the 'I hate Peter' syndrome as well. (Project worker)

The only way I could carry on was to keep my distance. *Everybody* had such strong feelings about the child, and *everybody* knows exactly what is right for him. (Local authority worker)

We felt we had been very naughty. I felt rejection – we'd deserved it. I saw us as the real naughties in the middle, who hadn't made any sort of effort. We had wasted all the resources. Maybe we needed counselling afterwards. But all their resources must go to the child. We coped. Perhaps I needed the reassurance we weren't unique. (Prospective parent)

In chapter 3 we referred to the problem of putting over our essentially positive appraisal of the work of the agency whilst reporting fully any criticisms and difficulties. The problem has been particularly acute in this chapter, since it is in the context of shared decision-making, in almost every case involving compromise on somebody's part, that difficulties are most likely to surface. Despite the stresses and painful feelings, the opinions expressed by the two sets of workers about each other were basically positive. Not surprisingly, reservations were more likely to be voiced when an introduction to a new family was unsuccessful.

In the next chapter we look at the social work in detail. Here we conclude with a sample of the many positive comments made by local authority field and residential workers about the work of the agency as a whole:

Our confidence in them was boosted by the speed and quality of the reports they send.

Our expectation of The Child Wants a Home is that we would get a good service. We would expect to have to put in less work with the family.

SUMMARY

In this chapter we have described the complex processes involved in the placement of 'special needs' children with new families. Although some of the difficulties are only relevant to placement by voluntary agencies, we concluded that most might also be encountered when specialist and area team workers from the same agency were working together. We have looked in detail at the various stages, finding that some are likely to be more difficult to manage than others. We found that the first meeting between the social worker for the child and the proposed new family and *their* social worker was especially fraught with difficulties.

We concluded that the complex process of bringing together a child with special needs and a new family can never be easy. From our detailed examination of these cases, viewed from the different perspectives, we have made suggestions about how some of the problems might be avoided or minimized.

9

The Nature of Social Work in Permanent Family Placement

I must say, one can get quite hysterical about finding families. My colleagues started making remarks about my being too involved. Which I think is quite dotty because how do you work hard at something unless you are committed. So easily these children can be left to drift. They don't drive you, so you have got to create a sense of drivenness from somewhere. In a funny way I don't find him a particularly attractive boy. But you don't work with somebody's history without getting very close.

(Social worker)

A back-seat driver can't make the decisions because they can't see what the front seat driver has seen. They are not the front seat driver and they don't know the front seat driver's capabilities.

(Adoptive mother)

We now take a closer look at the nature of the social work service offered to members of the natural families and the new families. We have already noted that most of the work with the children and their natural parents before placement was undertaken by the local authority field or residential workers, occasionally in partnership with the project worker. The social work tasks during the introductory period were shared, and the social work after placement was almost entirely the responsibility of the project workers. As in other areas of our study, our 'evidence' comes from a variety of sources. Sometimes it is contradictory, and on more than one occasion individuals contradicted themselves at different stages in the process. We collected a mass of material on the subject of social work practice – a subject which was equally fascinating to the social workers and to their 'consumers'. We hope that we have selected from it in a fair and balanced way, and regret in writing this chapter, even more than the others, that we did not have time to interview any members of natural families other than siblings placed together. We did, however, learn much from the perceptive comments of some of the children who shared their parents and their homes with new brothers and sisters – enough to suggest that this particular group of consumers can be a rich source of constructively critical comment on social work practice.

SOCIAL WORK WITH NATURAL FAMILIES

Our evidence about social work with natural parents comes mostly from CWAH files and from the residential and field social workers, but also from previous foster parents and sometimes from those members of the new families who met natural parents or siblings. For most of the local authority workers interviewed, their main concerns in dealing with natural parents were to clarify the legal position, to obtain agreement for permanent placement and for publicity, and in some cases to obtain consent to adoption. Only five of the 14 families involved in our main study were being offered a social work service directed to their own needs as opposed to the needs of their children and the new families, although two others (those who visited their children after placement) had been offered emotional support over a period of years, mainly by residential workers. Since our fieldwork was completed, the Adoption Agency Regulations have been revised; they now emphasize that parents whose children may be adopted should receive a counselling service in their own right.

Those who did offer a service to natural parents described vividly the pressures this imposed upon them. Principally the problem in trying to meet the needs both of natural parents and of children to be placed was one of conflicting pressures, but it was made worse by different time scales, as the following comments by a worker interviewed during an introduction suggest:

I feel emotionally drained. Though you are aiming for adoption you cannot say when is the right time. Because of the three-way pull – the conflicting pulls on Anne of her foster parents, her natural parents and family members, and the adoptive parents – it has been difficult to keep it moving at a pace which is right for getting her settled in her new home, but at the same time gives me time to work properly with the rest of the family. There were so many people to work with who all live so far apart. I was conscious of not allowing her to be left 'in limbo' because of everyone else's needs. But in the long run, if they can help her to move – if I can do it properly and keep them all in touch with what is going on – that will be better for her.

The other major problem faced by social workers also working with the natural parents was how and when to introduce the idea of adoption. In several cases, especially where there had been abuse or neglect but was still some degree of mutual attachment, parents were able to express their continued concern while also accepting that it would be in the child's interest to have a permanent new family. Workers who had supported the family through committal to care and the difficult processes which led to this conclusion, and who were probably in some cases working hard to make sure that other children of the family could have the advantages of 'permanence' by remaining with their natural parents, found discussion of adoption difficult. Some workers decided to wait until the child was well settled before raising the possibility. However, there was some uneasiness about not being totally honest with the parents, especially if the placement they were aiming for was a straight adoptive one rather than a foster placement which might grow into adoption. A local authority worker reported of one family,

They have changed dramatically. They are living together happily and all the children except Alan are now out of care. But there is no way Alan can go back. I am absolutely sure, and they have made no noises about it. I had adoption in mind. It's only a matter of the terms you use. They have agreed that he is to be placed in a permanent home and have agreed to publicity. They say things like, 'When he is settled perhaps we will have him back for the odd weekend.' I haven't spelled out the word adoption because adoption to them means signing away your rights to the child permanently. This is where we could come against a block. But his mother can see what is right for him.

Those social workers who were still involved with natural families tended to have a more difficult task than others in dealing with new parents, whose complex feelings about the child's previous life sometimes led them to transfer onto the social worker any feelings of hostility they had towards the birth parents. In the view of the new families, the main functions of social work with the natural parents were to help to make any continued contact between them and their offspring as satisfactory as possible, and, more often, to tie up any legal loose ends so that adoption could proceed. When social workers failed to do this as quickly as the new parents desired, any previous good opinion they might have had of them was wiped out by their increased anxiety at what they saw as unnecessary delay. On the other hand, when, as sometimes happened, a different social worker was involved with the natural family, this might create less tension but it could be even less satisfactory in expediting the adoption process.

Most of the local authority workers in this study either did not believe in the desirability or possibility of continued contact with natural parents, or did not believe in it strongly enough to place it high on their list of needs to be met for a placement to be considered appropriate. In some cases it was the new parents who insisted on the need for either initial contact or continued contact with natural parents, despite the difficulties this sometimes made for them. In other cases it was project workers who reassured local authority workers that continued contact was desirable and possible. There is limited evidence from this study and more especially from the work of Fratter and her colleagues (1982) that determined social workers can achieve permanent placement with parental contact.

Distance often made this difficult, but we felt that *project* workers could in more cases have had some contact with natural parents after placement – at least, as one project worker put it, 'to tell them at first hand about the placement'. 16 of the 21 children placed were not totally rejected by their parents, even though they were not able to offer them a home. A joint visit by the project worker and the local authority worker after placement could in some cases have been helpful both for the natural parents themselves and for the children and their new parents, and have given the project workers a clearer idea of the natural family's position once the placement process had been completed. They might have discussed with the family whether there was any further role they could play to help the child; how they might feel about the child initiating contact after reaching maturity; whether they would like to receive another photo of the child; whether it would be in the child's interest to receive birthday cards; and so on. Whilst local authority workers were able to do all these things, the project workers, because of their greater awareness of how relationships were developing in the new family, might have been able to handle such issues with greater sensitivity. From our interviews with some of the older children who had not remained in contact and still had unresolved feelings about natural parents and siblings, we felt that this issue would recur over the years. Our interviews with project workers led us to conclude that they sometimes did not know enough about how things were with the natural family. In only one case did a project worker visit a natural parent after the children were fairly well settled, and this was considered helpful by the new parents and the children.

Although we did not interview natural parents, we were left with an uneasy feeling that in most cases the standard of work with them fell far short of that with the children or the new parents.

WORK WITH THE NEW FAMILIES BY LOCAL AUTHORITY WORKERS

Most of the work with the new families was undertaken by the project workers, and we have already noted that, where a different project worker had done preparatory work with the child, she usually, following agency policy, withdrew during the introductory stage, leaving the family's worker to support the placement. In the eyes of the families, and especially of the children, a clear line was drawn between the project worker, who was the *parents'* social worker, and the local authority worker, who was the *child's* social worker. Most of the new parents had mixed feelings about social workers. They tended to view them, either as a breed or individually, with suspicion or apprehension. Ten of the 14 families expressed negative feelings about social workers or social work agencies, sometimes because, as noted earlier, they tended as a group to believe in the importance of 'standing on your own two feet'; sometimes because social workers had turned them down or kept them waiting as potential foster or adoptive parents, or had dealt less than sensitively with a request for help by themselves or someone they knew.

I haven't got a lot of time for social workers. They let us down before. To me they know nothing and don't want to know anything. (Father)

Janet was lucky to have him as a social worker. He was kindly and warm. Not at all social workerish. (Mother)

Well, what can you expect of social workers? They are run by the government, aren't they? (Father)

I thought, how am I going to manage with a social worker around. I've never had a social worker before with my other children. (Mother)

Only two of the families had generally positive feelings about social workers as a professional group, and two we considered to be neutral. In a sample of foster or adoptive parents of Down's children, Gath (1983) noted a similar general, negative view of social workers. However, they also tended to be inconsistent, usually making positive comments about the local authority workers early in the placement, but becoming more critical as time went on. This shows how cautions one must be in interpreting consumer studies of social work based on only one interview with the client. We have already noted in chapter 8 how impressed we were by the skill, determination and concern with which most local authority workers tackled the task of finding new families for the children. We were therefore unwilling to accept totally at face value the generally negative view of them and of their work expressed by the families, and hypothesized that this splitting of good and bad served for some as a means of coping with stress, as it often did for the children themselves. In this way the project worker could remain the dependable, caring person and difficulties could be blamed on the local authority or the child's past life, as represented by the social worker. This is not to deny that there were examples of bad practice, and, certainly, one of the reasons why some parents changed their view of their local authority social workers is that the service offered was not as efficient as they had expected and in their opinion did not meet the needs of the case.

In our earlier interviews families spoke warmly of the concern which local authority workers showed for the children; of their gratitude for a worker's efforts in seeking the right placement for a child; and of gratification that the worker had chosen *them* as a suitable family. Perhaps the children's honeymoon period also extended to the social workers who had brought them. Although only three workers paid more than one or two visits after placement, and none set out explicitly to provide a social work service to the new family as opposed to helping the child over the transition, six families thought that the local authority worker cared about them as a family, and about half thought that the child really did matter to the worker. As time passed, however, the former workers became associated in the minds of new parents with the child's unhappy past, and they became inclined, especially since they rarely saw these workers, to remember only negative things about them. This tendency was reinforced by the fact that some of the children who had been attached to their local authority workers felt a need to reject them, along with the past they represented. In one case a mother had told us, 'His social worker was very clued up on him, and cared a lot about him. That's what I liked about him. Talking to him about Dan helped us more than anything else. He knew exactly what sort of home he needed'; but six months later she could say of the same worker, 'He is an unnecessary evil. Is it necessary that he comes down here at a cost of £20 a day?'

Also, as time wore on and problems began to show themselves, the local authority social worker provided a convenient scapegoat, especially if, as was usually the case with children in care, there were problems about payment of allowances or 'special needs' grants, or obtaining adoption consents.

We analysed the social work service in terms of the relationship offered and the tasks of social work, comparing the perceptions of the families, the children and the social workers about what these should be and what was actually the case. In order to gain more information on the nature of the relationship between workers, parents and children, we asked a series of questions about whether social workers and parents liked each other, whether they had similar values and views about bringing up children, and whether they thought they 'mattered' to each other. Studies of effectiveness in social work (Truax and Carkhuff, 1967) have indicated that accurate empathy and genuineness are important components, and consumer studies (Mayer and Timms, 1970; Sainsbury, 1975, 1983; Thoburn, 1980; Rees and Wallace, 1982) have confirmed this conclusion but added that the *efficient* provision of appropriate services is seen by consumers as an essential component of a *caring* service. Accurate empathy is judged by clients in terms of what social workers do, as well as what sort of people they are, and our study confirmed this. In the early stages, local authority workers tended to be well thought of because they 'delivered the goods': by providing the child after months or even years of preparation and waiting; by providing information (usually accurate); and by the help they gave during the introductory period, often by acting as escort or providing equipment or grants.

Families tended to see the role of the local authority workers in much more limited terms than that of the project workers and most were well aware of this. One local authority worker commented, 'The family sees me as a little bit irrelevant.'

However, there was usually agreement that it was appropriate for the local authority workers to have a role with the *children* – tailing off after the introductory period; to provide a link with previous caretakers and the natural family; and to make sure that the practical tasks of the local authority were efficiently carried out. It is interesting that few of the parents mentioned the role of the local authority worker as decision-maker, even though the worker was present at the planning meeting and at the six-monthly reviews for children in care. Where the role was acknowledged, it was in terms of decision about financial or practical help. Although six workers thought they had a role in giving advice to parents, usually about ways of meeting the child's needs or of handling behaviour problems during the settling-in period, none of the families thought this an appropriate role for the local authorty workers. Their role was seen in terms of tasks rather than relationships.

The roles which the local authority workers felt they needed to fulfil were precisely those which the parents found most difficult. In particular they resented being given advice, and the supervisory or decision-making role of the workers:

We don't like being watched. We feel on trial.

With her, if I start to talk to her about him, she thinks I am asking her advice. She might suggest I should do things differently from what I intend to do.

Local authority workers were aware of this difficulty, and their usual method of working through problems – getting to know the family well enough to become a real person to them, so that differences could be safely aired – was precluded in most cases because of project policy and distance. One remarked of a particular family, 'It became more difficult working with them once they had the child. They were not very good at taking advice. Sometimes they make it clear my visit is a nuisance. It is not to do with personalities. It is to do with roles.'

A final reason why local authorty workers were likely to be 'marginalized' lay in the sort of people the new parents were. We have already noted that they tended to be independent people who had an antipathy to social workers and bureaucracy. They were also natural givers rather than takers. They were grateful to the local authority workers for giving them a child but were not comfortable in this role. With the project workers their role was that of the giver – of a home to a child who needed it and who they knew was not easy to care for – and this was a role with which they felt much more at ease.

THE PROJECT WORKERS' ROLES WITH THE NEW FAMILIES

The project workers also had to overcome the antipathy felt by most families towards social workers as a group, but they had the advantage of getting to know them through the preparation period and, being members of a voluntary agency, of not, at least in law, being the final arbiters of whether the placement should continue. There was no evidence of the project workers playing down their decision-making role or colluding with the tendency of parents to see them as good and the local authority workers as bad. However, the families themselves frequently explained their high opinion of the project workers in terms of their playing down their authority role. One mother commented, 'We agree with what she [the project worker] says. She doesn't say much. She is not domineering. She doesn't ever strike me as a social worker.'

In general, families were positive about the inquirers' groups and preparation groups, though they were sometimes critical of the material used, especially the American films. The aspect of preparation groups which was especially valued was the opportunity to meet foster and adoptive families. Families differed about how much they felt they had learned, but all were unanimous in their praise of the way they were welcomed by the agency at this stage. A father told us, 'We liked the agency. We felt welcome. We felt we could go through this experience with them.'

The preparation groups also provided an opportunity for parents to get to know all the project workers, which helped them to form a trusting relationship with the agency as a whole and feel able to speak to other workers in the future. The intimacy of a small voluntary agency is undoubtedly one of its strengths and one which local authorities undertaking permanent placement work would do well to replicate.

The home study and approval process was the stage which the families and social workers found most difficult, although both stressed that having gone through this process together made it possible for them to trust each other once the child had been placed. Project workers saw their role at this stage as a complex one, combining as it did elements of teaching, assessing, supporting, and forming a relationship. The agenda for the families was much simpler: to persuade the worker that they were suitable people to parent a child, and to get on with deciding which sort of child. Thus, they almost all complained of the time the home study took, and this was especially the case if the family had responded to the request for a home for a specific child. One mother said, 'We felt it was going on so long that someone else would get her first.'

Several families had been through it all before with other agencies, some to be rejected and some accepted. For those who had been rejected, usually childless couples wishing to adopt, the process was even more stressful. A mother told us, 'We felt uneasy and resentful with her [the project worker] at first. All those probing questions', while a father confessed, 'We breathed a sigh of relief at the end of each session.'

Most accepted the home study with good grace, sometimes seeing it as a sort of initiation rite which had to be gone through to prove one's worth – if you could survive that, you would have the tenacity to take anything a child could throw at you. As one mother put it, 'It's incredible what you have to go through. But I can understand it. We told them everything. We decided there was no point in being anything but honest. If you aren't honest, other things can crop up.'

Some families commented on the patience of the social workers in helping them to think about the sort of child who would fit into their home:

It was a strain on us. You think all sorts of things. But they took a lot of time understanding what we could cope with and didn't try to palm us off with a child we couldn't cope with. She made time, even if she didn't have it. She didn't use to say 'I have to go now.' She didn't rush you.

Other families were quietly confident, and set themselves the task of patiently explaining to the social worker that they knew precisely what they were doing:

She did her social worker bit. She may not have agreed with our views, or understood us completely, but she understood us enough to put us fairly to her committee. (Mother)

They felt very confident in their ability. I don't think it's unusual for families to find the home study very tedious. I found it difficult to delve into their past. They are 'here and now' people. They found it tedious to have to convince someone else. They were so sure. (Project worker)

Project workers adopted different styles with different people:

I like to level with people. To a degree I am an expert. I ordered her to go to the Adult Training Centre and refused to visit again until she had been.

I need to spend a lot of time there. She needed her self-confidence boosting after rejection by the adoption agency.

Although most of the families commented on the skill and sensitivity of the workers, some were more mixed in their reactions:

For the parents it is really difficult – to be offering and then to be torn apart. People have to own up to the bad bits in themselves or in their families in the past. (Project worker)

Who are these people to play God and say who should have a parent and who should not? They are depriving a child of a natural childhood, and it's every child's right to have someone to care for them. (Mother)

After the home study was completed, some parents were linked with a child quickly, but for others it was some while before they could decide that a particular child might be the right one for them. This could again be a difficult time. One mother commented, 'You spend your time waiting for letters or phone calls. You don't like to ring. It seems impatient.'

The social workers had to find the right balance between encouraging the parents to maintain their interest by visiting and talking about the children in the 'Be My Parent' book, and not seeming to put pressure on the parents. A mother remarked disapprovingly, 'They kept bringing piles of papers of children to sort out what we wanted.' In the event an unsuccessful introduction was made in this case, and it became clear that what the family wanted was precisely what the agency did not have within its power to place – a healthy baby.

Once a family had been accepted by the panel, the relationship between them and the worker took a leap forward, and one worker felt that only a this stage were most families really ready to learn about and discuss freely the implications for all family members of integrating a new child into their home.

By the time a child was placed, the social work relationship was well established. Although the styles and personalities of the workers differed, their basic philosophy and methods were very similar. In essence, they believed that, once a family had been approved and a child placed, the role of the project worker was to emphasize the unity of the new family and support the parents in their parenting role. As one worker put it, 'They need a good, solid, rock-like "keep it all together" sort of person. A general enabler, accepter, encourager, a professional friend.'

The degree of congruence between the views of families and of the project workers themselves about what their role ought to be is quite striking, and undoubtedly contributed to the success of the placements and the general satisfaction of the families. The following comments illustrate just how similar were the views held about the role of the worker:

I always get across to people, for instance at school, that they want to be treated as a family, so please go through them and not me. (Project worker)

The most productive and helpful thing for our particular family is to let us get on with it. Not because we are arrogant, but because they can't know what it is really like. (Mother)

You've got to do things their way. It's their family. (Project worker)

She realizes that if we are going to be happy with him we have to do it our way. (Father)

You mustn't be scared of letting people have their heads. It's misunderstanding the bonding process to think you can control and direct how they parent. During the home study we *do* judge the way they bring up their children. Once we have placed we don't judge them. (Project worker)

Before going on to consider the various roles and tasks of the project workers in more detail, we shall consider the nature of the relationship between parents and workers. We quoted above the project worker who described herself as a 'professional friend'. Table 9.1 shows that families were more likely than workers to describe the relationship as one of friendship, but interestingly the same was also true of perceptions of the relationship as one of colleagues. A mother told us, 'We feel more like friends. It isn't us and them. We were guinea-pigs trying a new way of adopting older children. We appreciated the efficiency and the back-up.'

Table 9.1 The role of the project social workers as seen by the workers and the parents (number of times mentioned)

Role	Project worker's opinion	New parents' opinion (13 families)
Child's escort	4	1
Child's friend	1	4
Negotiator for child with family	5	5
Someone who will make sure clothes, pocket money, etc., are provided for child	8	2
Helper for child	5	8
Therapist for child	5	2
Family's friend	4	9
Colleague	3	6
Helper for family	12	8
Advice-giver	8	11
Therapist for family	2	3
Link with previous caretaker	7	2
Link with natural family	3	4
Negotiator with placing authority	11	8
Someone who will make sure family receives allowances, etc.	11	8
Someone who will check that things are all right for the child	11	8
Supervisor for family	8	7
Inspector	2	2
Decision-maker	8	4

We hypothesized that shared values would make it easier for social workers to delegate responsibility to the families and resist the temptation to 'back-seat drive', and found some support for this in the answers to our questions about values and about whether parents and social workers liked each other and had similar views about how to bring up children. We found few cases where worker and parents disagreed strongly on fundamental points or expressed dislike of each other. This was in part because both parties made a big effort to find common ground and things they liked about each other, and occasionally they had to make an effort to play down aspects of the other party which were inclined to annoy them. Parents were most inclined to complain about bossiness and unpredictability, which was particularly difficult to cope with given the powerful position of the project worker in the decision-making process. One mother told us,

The bossiness didn't help. It made it worse. Social workers have their ups and downs. Sometimes she over-reacts. But she is in a position of power. I know if she says do X we do it, because we want Ellen. She has an abrasive quality. But is that us? Does it mean we annoy her when other people wouldn't?

On the other hand, parents and workers tended to be united by their concern for children and this was sometimes expressed in religious terms:

She is really excellent. She has Peter's welfare at heart and wants what is best for him. (Father)

The fact that we have the same Christian values helps. It makes them seem comfortable with me. (Project worker)

Parents and workers also tended to place value on the efficient use of time and resources:

We got so fed up with the local authority worker being late. It is awfully difficult having social workers keep coming to one's home. They must know that for heaven's sake. The project worker was efficient. Which is what we wanted. I couldn't have stood an agency that dilly-dallied and kept you hanging around as some of them do. (Father)

She is a 'no nonsense' sort of person. So am I. We were customers for one of her children and that is what they are there for. (Father)

The following comments summarize the views of project workers and parents about shared values.

As people, I share a lot of their values. So in that sense I am not having to make a lot of the adjustments I have to with other people. (Project worker)

We don't have exactly the same values. But it's enough to make us sympathetic friends. (Father)

It doesn't matter if values are different if you are not telling them how to parent. But if you have the same values it does help you to understand. (Project worker)

If you do want to do something, you have to spend quite a bit of time explaining what your values are, why you are doing it, before you can make the point. (Mother)

Sometimes I like them, and sometimes they irritated me. I sometimes think they are pulling the wool over my eyes. It's easier if you can like the kind of people they are. As a family, they are probably better when I am out of the way. (Project worker)

Sometimes differences in outlook were related to social class (most obviously when it came to child-rearing practices such as smacking children):

·She is a bit 'uppity' sometimes. (Father)

You can't expect to get on with all the families because of differences in culture patterns. Sometimes I feel very much university graduate, middle-class Tory voter. (I'm not most of these.) But I'm surprised how well I melt into the family. (Project worker)

Parents were more inclined than workers to think that they had similar views on how to bring up children, but this can be explained by the project workers' view that their role was to support the parents in their own method of caring. One worker described herself as 'a bit like litmus paper – a bit chameleon-like'. Although several parents echoed the comments made by clients interviewed in other studies that social workers who did not have children of their own could not possibly give advice about how to bring up children, this was rarely said in a spirit of complaint. As we shall see later when we consider the advice-giving role, most parents were not looking to the workers for detailed advice about how to look after children, and were sometimes pleased to have a reason for rejecting it if it was given. One father remarked, 'She doesn't understand what it is like to have children. They always think they know. They think to themselves, "Oh I wouldn't let mine do that." '

For parents, the most important factor in determining whether the relationship with the social worker was seen as helpful was whether the worker cared about them – whether they mattered to her – and this was often judged in terms of the sort of service offered. Almost all the families thought that they and the child mattered to the worker, and referred to particular actions which convinced them of this. They especially appreciated being given the workers' home 'phone numbers, even though no family used the number other than in response to serious difficulties. A mother commented, 'We appreciated the gesture of giving us her home phone number. We wouldn't use it though. They are a superb agency. They give so much support to the foster parents. Our social worker has been with us all the way.'

Visits for the project workers followed very similar patterns. They visited weekly or fortnightly during the first six months, and then approximately monthly or two-monthly, but stepping up the frequency with the agreement of the parents if there was a reason to do so. All the parents thought that the frequency of visits was about right. Visits were by appointment and arranged well in advance. Sometimes the worker phoned between visits, and sometimes a parent phoned, but it was a point of principle to most parents not to phone unless it was unavoidable. One project worker remarked on this, 'They never phone between visits. They don't believe in it. Chris has done the most terrible things. But they won't. That is why I had to go weekly. I knew they wouldn't phone, even if he burned the house down!'

Workers said that the family did matter to them and considered that in ten of the fourteen cases they mattered to the parents:

It is a truly professional relationship. But we have similar values, and I think we know we are fond of ach other and there is trust there.

They want you to be a friend, except you aren't quite. But nor are you the detached professional. You are somewhere between. It is like walking a tightrope. But I don't know how you can do this job if you aren't involved up to a point.

This concern did not always get across to the parents, and if it did not, workers tended to be thought less well of. One father told us, 'Jenny, to her, is just part of her job, and that is that. You should be concerned, and you should have your heart in the right place, if you are going to do right by the kids. If they just represent a job to you, you can't show much feeling towards them.' This was one of only two cases where there was any significant disagreement between the worker's and the parents' view of their relationship, and in part this stemmed from a professional decision not to make a close relationship with the child, which was interpreted as lack of concern.

To summarize, there was substantial agreement between workers and parents as to the nature of their relationship. They were 'professional friends' who genuinely mattered to each other, colleagues embarked on an enterprise where each had a role to play. The parents had the major role of caring for the child. What, then, in more detail did the social workers do? We shall consider this in terms of practical services, the statutory aspects of the role, and problem-solving aspects.

Practical help

We found neither disagreement nor dissatisfaction in the area of practical help. Taking a handicapped child or a sibling group into their homes involved considerable expense for some families. In three cases house extensions were built, and in two other cases there was a move to a bigger house. Project workers were heavily involved in helping families with these costs, either by negotiating with the local authority or by raising funds from charitable sources. They also helped with applications for state benefits such as attendance and mobility allowance or supplementary benefit, and, in the later stages, adoption allowances and legal fees for contested adoptions. This help was greatly appreciated by the parents, who were not the sort of people who found it easy to ask for practical help. The worker's role as negotiator with the placing authority at times became that of advocate for the family, a role which was sometimes resented. One local authority worker considered that the project worker was colluding with the parents' unrealistic demands on the authority's limited resources and should have been helping them to understand appropriate procedures. The other form of practical help often mentioned was with transport at the introductory stage, both for the child and in order to facilitate meetings with members of the natural family. As is so often the case, practical help was also an important avenue to cementing relationships, in that the emotional support was vitally important at such meetings. In one case the round tour to meet all the important members of the natural family was recalled vividly. The mother commented, 'If she [the worker] didn't know us after twenty-four hours, going round the country meeting all the relatives, she never would.'

Supervision

Social workers were more likely to mention their statutory role as supervisors or decision-makers than were families. This was probably because, as we have already noted, workers deliberately played down this role in order to help the children develop trust in their new parents right from the start. At the planning meeting the project workers insisted on delegating to foster families the maximum amount of responsibility permissible under the Boarding-Out Regulations. All families were given letters stating that they had power to sign consents for emergency treatment or routine school trips, and children were rarely seen on their own for any length of time. (It is increasingly being suggested that practice and procedures which stress the local authority's decision-making role at the expense of that of the new parents may breed the very insecurity which one is seeking to avoid: see Triseliotis, 1983; and, most recently, in their study of long-term foster care, Rowe et al., 1984). Our interviews with parents and children suggested that this strategy was successful, in that by the two-year stage we detected no anxiety amongst the parents that the placement would be ended by anyone other than them or the child. Some families did, however, mention the supervisory role of the workers, sometimes welcoming it, sometimes accepting it as appropriate, and sometimes feeling uncomfortable about it whilst accepting its inevitability:

We are on trial when she comes. On our best behaviour. It is a fear of being found to be failing.

Our daughter stayed away when the social worker came because she was afraid she might say something wrong.

She is someone to talk things over with – a supervisor.

She has to come every two months. I talk to her like a neighbour. I prefer her not to quote the book at me.

In the early stages of the placement the decision-making role deterred some families from talking over problems which they would have liked to have discussed. When asked to whom they would turn for advice about the child, only five mentioned the project worker, the others saying they would go to members of the family or to friends. None said that they would turn to other foster or adoptive parents, perhaps emphasizing their preferred identity as an 'ordinary' family. However, at the later stages two families who were hitting problems talked about the help they got from talking to other adoptive parents. The project workers were aware that families tended not to talk to them about even fairly serious difficulties, preferring to handle them as they cropped up and usually tell the workers when they visited:

I think what they tell me is true, whether they tell me the whole truth, I don't know. I don't get to hear everything that happens – even things I think I ought to know. But that is how it is. I knew it would be like that. I have to work with it.

I worry about some families, the way they are doing things. But I don't criticize. I have to find the most comfortable way of helping. My skill is doing it in a way they can accept it.

Sometimes workers did not succeed in hiding their unease, and reacted in such a way as to make families wary in future.

She is very much a social worker. Sometimes I want to talk about things I am a bit nervous about. But sometimes when I have chatted over very ordinary things they have snowballed into great mountains, and grown out of all proportion, which I think is a little bit sad. It makes you tighten up and you tend to guard every word. So I wouldn't share little things that I would be glad to chat over sometimes. They always look out for reasons. We would like to handle things ourselves and not worry about reasons. Then the problem is always referred to long after it's been dealt with. (Mother)

Sometimes we let off steam about something. She will get a bee in her bonnet and go over the top about it, and have forgotten about it next time. Because of her power, it is very disorientating and upsetting. (Father)

Sometimes parents felt it important to their developing relationship with the youngster that they should not be seen as 'telling tales', and would make a point of saving up any difficulties until a routine visit and then playing down their significance, merely describing whatever had happened and how they had handled it. One mother told us,

> I don't call Janet in. I handle it myself. I tell her afterwards. You have got no social worker to turn to for your own kiddies. They say, 'Are you going to tell Janet?' I say, 'What do you think?' Usually I tell her, but it's between us. I tell her to keep it between us. Sometimes I tell them I'm going to tell Janet, and she talks to them when I'm there.

The formal decision-making process was the statutory review, at which new parents were always present and encouraged to play a major role. A minority of the families saw reviews in a positive light. Most thought they were unnecessary, and others thought them harmful, largely because of the bad effect they had on the children, a subject we return to in the next chapter.

Although one of the original aims of the project was to try to use groups not only at the preparation stage but also as a means of offering continued support, there was no formal group work after children were placed. However, two 'family get-togethers' were held and attended by about three-quarters of the families. Parents enjoyed these social events, but told us that they would not see any value in regular groups. Some families helped as 'veterans' with preparation groups, and welcomed the opportunity to be of use to the agency. For some this helped to give them a sense that what they were doing was worthwhile – particularly useful if the child was going through a difficult and unrewarding stage.

After a child had been adopted, formal visits by the project workers ended, but in all cases they were welcome visitors and made an agreement with the families about whether they should visit regularly every six months or so or leave things more flexible. For most of the families who had adopted, the guardian *ad litem* played a useful but minor role. However, in one contested case he played an important role at a time when the parents were dissatisfied with the work of the local authority worker because of delays in the adoption process, and felt anxious about the authority role of the project worker. The arrival on the scene of a knowledgeable but neutral worker at a rather fraught time for the family was greatly appreciated by them. In another case the guardian was described as unhelpful. The father complained, 'She really hurt us by raising all the problems after we had convinced ourselves it would be all right. She didn't know what she was talking about. They are teaching fish to swim.'

Problem-solving

Since most parents played down the role of the social worker as someone to give advice on how to look after children, we were rather surprised that it was the role most often ticked on the check list. When we pursued the matter it became clear that the workers did tend to give advice on a variety of subjects, some aspects of it more welcome than others. Advice about day-to-day parenting was least valued: 'Her role of telling us what to do. We very much dislike this role', one father remarked.

On the other hand advice and information about the legal system and adoption procedures were most welcome. Advice about the special needs of the child was also welcomed by some parents, though not others. One mother told us, 'I think I know more than she does.'

Those who worked on an intuitive level complained that they were always given reasons and theories which they found unhelpful. The parents of Down's children or physically handicapped children quickly became more expert in the condition of their child than the worker, and preferred to turn to the appropriate parent self-help group, the specialist teacher or their medical practitioner. Most parents did welcome the teaching started during the preparation groups about the special problems of children who have spent long periods in care, and methods of helping them overcome the symptoms of deprivation. However, the workers were careful not to put themselves in the role of experts, thus undermining the confidence and competence of the parents. One of the project workers consisdered that not having been the child's worker before placement was a help here:

If the social worker has not prepared the child for placement, she doesn't become the expert with knowledge of the child which the family hasn't got. She is the facilitator for the child and the family to work together, not the expert on the child. It is a style of work which makes the social worker less important.

Another commented, 'What I have to offer is not child care expertise. It is interpretation of what is common to the process of building a new family. That lying and regression happen in nearly every case, for instance.'

More important than advice to the families, however, was the role of listener: 'I am a listener', said one project worker. 'Then I help her to work out how she is going to handle it. I think it would be destructive to do direct work with Mary myself.'

For this reason, although social work practice was informed by the theories of family therapy, all except one of the workers saw their main role as giving time to the parents on their own. Sometimes they would work jointly with one or both parents and a child, perhaps undertaking life story work, making family trees or using dolls or puppets to help explore sensitive feelings. The following comments reflect project workers' views of their roles:

Mrs Dunn is a thinking person. She enjoys weighing it up. My words are always taken seriously. They weigh up what I say. She tells me how she has done it, or presents a problem and we tackle it together.

You help them to ventilate their sadness. Then you bring in your knowledge. You don't talk it. You demonstrate it in the work you do.

It is a question of confidence building. You give them the tools, books to read, etc. Ideas grow in the discussion.

This style of work was welcomed by the parents, and enabled them, either alone or taking a major role but alongside the worker, to undertake skilled and imaginative therapy with the children who needed it. In only two cases did workers describe themselves as therapists for the family, and this was mentioned three times by parents. On occasions some of the families were placed under so much stress that more direct help with specific problems of family relationships became necessary. This did present problems in that the change of role from colleague to therapist was not easily accomplished, nor were families immediately willing to seek help from another agency, such as a family psychiatry clinic. A project worker commented on one case,

But when there *were* problems, I didn't allow them to have problems. Maybe they were fed up with all this confidence I had in them. It's hard to pull back from the role of co-worker to the social worker–client thing. It's hard to make that switch. We lurched from problem to problem.

In each case the project workers planned out their work so as to provide what they considered to be the most appropriate service in the way which the family and child would find most acceptable. One observed, 'They don't like social workers. They think we are all fools. In this case I couldn't help the child until the foster parents were ready. I don't like seeing children in distress when I could do something about it. But I had to wait.' We sometimes wondered where the dividing line lay between planning and manipulation, but were consoled by the fact that families could be equally adept at devising strategies to get what they wanted out of the project worker or local authority worker.

SUMMARY

Families tended to rate the quality of social work offered by local authority workers less highly than that offered by project workers. However, we had doubts about taking this assessment totally at face value. Some parents' views as expressed to us changed over time, even when there had been no contact with a worker in the intervening period, and we considered that in some cases there were psychological mechanisms operating. Thus, although some negative comments about local authority workers, as about project workers, were justified, we considered that families and children were not always the most reliable witnesses in this respect. Our assessment was of a usually high standard of service from local authority workers, coupled with hard work, enthusiasm and determination to find a new family. The least adequate area was work with natural families.

Perhaps the best way of characterizing the social work after placement is in terms of consultation. The parents wanted and, for the most part, received the sort of service which a social worker asks of a team leader. They accepted the workers' ultimate authority, but had confidence that the authority delegated to them as parents would not be interfered with unless this was necessary in the interest of the child. Reassured by this, they wanted regular opportunities to describe their activities, explain their difficulties, explore their ideas for alternative ways of handling them, consider other suggestions and receive offers of help in any joint work to be done. They wanted to share their happy moments and successes, receive praise and share pleasure. For this to happen they needed to feel valued and for all members of the family to be cared about. Finally, they needed to know that in a crisis competent help would be speedily available to them. A project worker described the relaxed approach at its best: 'Mrs Sanders bakes cakes and we sit down for a long talk. She enjoys two hours of introspection and reflection. Who doesn't! She is a thinking person, a colleague. She tells me how she has done it, or presents a problem, and we tackle it together.'

10

Social Work with the Children

Later he said to me, 'I thought as I was going to school today, oh good, Pat is coming and she will sort things out.' He meant I would get him to say what was worrying him.
(Project worker about eight-year-old Philip)

He tries to shut out the past. He nearly tore up a postcard she sent him. He said one day, 'I hate her', but the next day he hoped she would visit soon.
(Foster mother talking about residential worker)

Whilst the local authority workers did most of the work with the natural parents, and the project workers were invariably the key workers with the new parents, work with the children was undertaken by both. Before placement the local authority field workers carried out the traditional social care planning and casework tasks, sometimes in partnership with a residential worker. After placement the local authority workers faded quickly from the picture, apart from reviews and, if there had been a close relationship, sending postcards and birthday cards. 'My photo in their life story book is how I see my future role,' said one such worker.

In chapter 8 we looked at the social care planning role of the workers; here we shall concentrate on the casework service offered. Whilst research studies still indicate that social work with children is not of a generally high standard, there is a growing body of literature on how to work with children in care who are joining new families (Littner, 1960; BAAF, 1977; Jewett, 1978, 1985; Fahlberg, 1981; Fitzgerald, 1982; Fratter, 1982; Curtis, 1983). Of particular relevance here are the papers written by the staff of Parents for Children (Sawbridge, 1983; Argent, 1984), because their work influenced many of the local authority and project workers in our study. Morris (1984) has argued that workers with children for whom permanent family placement may be appropriate should slow down and take the time to listen carefully to what the child has to say about the plan. She is critical of a 'tendency towards omnipotence' which she notes in some workers, who give insufficient priority to ascertaining the child's wishes and feelings. 'In the rush for security the child's need for continuity with his family may be lost, and his identity shattered' (p. 18). Fitzgerald (1982) and Fratter and her colleagues (1982) have described the opportunities open to the residential worker to assess and prepare children. Lynch and Roberts (1982), writing about children who have been abused, some of whom came into care, have stressed the need for medical, neurological and psychological assessments. We have already commented in chapter 8 that the children in our study were offered a caring and skilled service by local authority workers who mostly saw themselves as child care specialists. Most were familiar with new developments in social work practice with children who are on the move, and used some of the methods outlined by the writers mentioned above, especially the technique of life story work. We shall not describe these techniques in detail, but comment on them and their effectiveness as perceived by the children, parents and residential and field social workers we interviewed.

As with the service offered to the new parents, we consider that offered to the children in terms of practical help, supervision and problem-solving, and in the context of the helping relationship. It was in the area of the relationship with the child that there was the biggest difference between, on the one hand, the residential and local authority field workers and, on the other, the project workers. This difference was the inevitable and appropriate consequence of different roles. Residential workers were acting as substitute parents either for short or long periods and could not fulfil that role without at least a limited attachment to the child. Field workers were fulfilling at least the planning and decision-making elements of the parental role, and the majority were involved sometimes over a period of years in 'holding' the child through a series of painful events and the loss of familiar people and places (Winnicott, 1965). It is not therefore surprising that they were more likely than the project workers to see themselves as the child's friend. Only four of the older children (two families) did not have a fairly close relationship with the field worker who initiated the referral for permanent placement, and these were in residential care and were attached to those caring for them. In one such case the field worker commented,

Picking up the pieces of the break of the second foster home was done at the children's home. I was very relieved they had the skills. I'm not in the business of visiting children every week just for the sake of keeping a relationship going. They've got people living with them to whom they can relate. My role is to step back from that.

The following comments are more representative of those workers who had known the children for some time:

I suppose there is a bit of me – I've known him for such a long time – understandably I have some emtional involvement with him.

I had been his social worker for seven years. I was the most permanent person he had.

You need to bond with the child to do work, but you need to be able to help him to move on.

In two cases project workers or new families felt that residential workers had made it difficult for children to move on, in part because of their emotional attachment, but in most cases they paid tribute to the way in which workers who obviously had emotional ties to their children as well as caring for their well-being were able to help them make the move.

The children's home was a good place to be for them. Bill said he couldn't meet the new family away from the children's home because Jenny [his key worker] wouldn't be there, so she came along with them. (Project worker)

I was very much against her being fostered. One day I was out for a walk and I said, 'You are being a very selfish woman. You are denying this child a family.' Then I carefully weighed it up and realized I had got an influence and I wasn't using it wisely in her case. We'd had so many broken fosterings here. You need to keep a distance at the end in fairness to the family. If the going gets rough she should talk to the new family, and not me. (Residential worker)

This last comment leads us on to some of the difficulties arising from close relationships between workers and children – mainly associated with the difficulty of ending the relationship in a helpful way. We found some indications of this in our interviews with the children and their new parents. Reactions to social workers after placement differed with the age of the child, but were otherwise sufficiently similar to merit comment. Three children under ten welcomed the continued interest of their local authority workers, and enjoyed seeing them when they visited, but did not seem to mind as the visits tailed off. The other children, and especially those who had known their workers for some time, had mixed feelings about visits after placement, and often difficult behaviour increased before, during or after a visit. Had we not interviewed the local authority and project workers, we might well have concluded from the interviews with the children and their parents that the children disliked their workers or had been given a poor service. Since we knew this was not the case, we hypothesized that the rejection of the local authority worker might be the result of one or more of the following factors.

1 Children were rejecting the workers along with their past, in order to help themselves make a fresh start: 'The children seemed very friendly with her [the worker] when we saw them at the children's home. But now, it's quite embarrassing. They hardly say two words to her' (mother).

2 In a concentrated attempt to relate to the new parents, all past relationships had to be blocked out: 'Bill cares for his social worker quite a lot, but he isn't going to show it' (project worker).

3 The child picked up the antipathy of the new parents to social workers in general, or this social worker in particular, and decided that rejection of the worker would win favour with the new parents: 'Mum's not too keen about her coming. I argue a lot with her when she comes' (teenage girl).

4 The child was angry with the social worker because of anger about the past with which she was associated: 'He hates her. He can't say why, only he hates her. It's her who made him move away from his family. He had to be angry with somebody and she was the person he chose to be angry with' (mother).

5 The child was attached to the social worker (and more often the residential worker) and was coping with feelings of separation by rejecting the worker, who now visited very infrequently: 'He was very rude to her. He doesn't like to

think that we think he worries about her. Instead of thinking about Andy, we are thinking about Mrs Jenkins. He gets upset after she has been. Swears in his sleep. It's not her personally. It's what she stands for' (mother).

6 The child was made anxious by a visit from the worker about whether this preceded another move: 'He doesn't like us talking to her. He always made a point of coming between us' (father).

Some of the families were gratified by these reactions, others embarrassed by them, and others tried to understand why there should be such strong reactions to apparently normally likable people who had obviously put a lot of effort into helping the child. A father observed of the relationship betwen one child and worker, 'He doesn't object to her personally. It's what she did to him – moving him.'

When we asked the children about their social workers' visits, it was mostly the fact that they had to be visited at all which they resented, since it emphasized their differentness, but this was obviously a confusing area for them. These visits aroused in them complex feelings which made them feel uncomfortable. A mother noted, 'She acts entirely differently when she's with her social worker. I think she even feels guilty herself afterwards. She said, "I was a bit of a beast to her, wasn't I?" '

When asked why he didn't want his local authority worker to visit, a teenage boy said, somewhat irrationally, 'She's all right I suppose. I saw her about twice a week at the children's home. When I said I didn't want her to find me another family she found one. I didn't want a family at first after it hadn't worked last time.' During the same interview he had told us how pleased he was to be there and how much he wanted to stay. Perhaps this is another example of gratitude being an uncomfortable emotion to sustain, or perhaps the problem was loss of face at being proved wrong.

The project workers, as we have noted above, stressed that they were the workers for the family. This, togther with the fact that, even when they worked with directly referred children before placement, they were not associated in the children's minds with, and potentially blamed for, the unhappy events of their early lives, meant that their visits were less troubling. Also they aimed to offer a relationship which allowed the children to feel confidence in them and trust them to help at difficult times, but which in no way competed with the new parents. Sometimes new parents interpreted this as lack of concern, but more often they appreciated it, and thought it was the best way of helping.

I try very hard not to see her on her own. I always see her with her mum or dad. (Project worker)

It is important to him that I am the family's worker. Alan accepts me because I am *their* worker. (Project worker)

It is so easy, especially for a childless couple, to fall into the competitive bit – 'Look what we are doing with the children. It's better than you can do.' So I don't have a significant relationship with the children. (Project worker)

The project worker isn't very good with children. We are grateful that she doesn't try to talk to him separately. (Mother)

It is perhaps significant that the only case where the project worker had a close relationship with a child was where a placement broke down and she had to help him deal with this and move into residential care and then on to another family. She reported, 'I have seen the change in the pattern with him. He used to throw his arms round me. He saw me as a person, not just another worker. It was very nice, on a recent visit, that he ignored me and went to throw his arms round his mum.'

In relation to the practical and problem-solving aspects of the work, we found less difference between the groups of workers. A technique used extensively throughout the placement process and afterwards was life story work. For most of the children it was returned to at strategic times, and the work was best undertaken in stages – by local authority workers, project workers or new parents, sometimes alone and sometimes together. One or two of the children enjoyed it, but most found it difficult, and some refused to enter into it in anything but a gruding way. A project worker noted of one child, 'He found it painful, and wouldn't admit that some of it happened. I had to write some bits because he wouldn't.' Sometimes a child would refuse to take part at one stage, but could be persuaded to so later. As one worker commented, 'You have to pick your moment. Do it when the child is ready.' One sibling might be ready for it while another might not, but, equally, he might not want to be left out of things or might be told things by his brother which were better told in the presence of a social worker or parent.

It was important to be clear about the purpose of life story books. If they were to be used to introduce a child to a new family, it might not be appropriate for everything from the past to be in them. One youngster wanted to talk about the painful bits in his early life, but would not allow them to go into his book. Referring to another case, a project worker enlarged on her technique:

We worked in the office, where we had access to the file. We forced Jenny to do the work. It was possibly not the right time for her, but it was the right time for Pat. I use simple language. I take parents and children as colleagues. I am quite blunt and convey the impression that I am quite unshockable, but understand why it is so horrible for them to be in care. I watch for physical signs – when to stop – when to feed them (we have an ample supply of chocolate biscuits) – when they want drinks. It is important to look competent throughout – to convey the message, 'No, I am not going to back off. It will be better after.'

The life story sessions when parents and workers joined together were opportunities for 'modelling', for the parents to learn skills for helping their children by observing the worker in action. Those parents who took part in these were very positive about the skills of the workers.

Life work was not the only therapeutic technique used with the children. Several social workers stressed their 'talking through' and 'debriefing' roles during the introductory stage, and found a good relationship was particularly useful at this stage in helping them recognize a change in the child's mood. Referring to a nine-year-old a project worker reported, 'I used "Teddy work" at the introduction and during the first month. I asked questions through Teddy. He was living in a fantasy world.'

The only stage where we felt that the work with the children was less than adequate was when it came to deciding what sort of home might be appropriate. This was particularly so with younger children or those who were mentally handicapped and were likely to think in concrete terms. Social workers used the technique of asking the children to make posters describing themselves and the sort of family they would like to live with. The children inevitably thought in terms of type of house, garden, children, pets and physical attractiveness of parents. Whilst the social workers saw this as a starting point, and did not feel that they should be bound by these suggestions, it was not uncommon for the children to feel that they had been promised that sort of family, and to feel disappointment when a family was suggested which did not fit their picture. We considered that it was a mistake for young children to be asked directly what sort of family they would like, and that more use could be made of psychological tests to gain a picture of the way in which the child was conceptualizing a new family, without running the risk of seeming to promise a particular sort of placement.

We also considered that this applied to the issue of adoption for the older children. If children had been promised adoption, they felt let down if offered a permanent home where there was love and security but they were not to be adopted, whereas those who had been promised security and family life without stress having been placed on the legal status seemed content to be fostered. Whilst one or two of the older children who were still being fostered at the end of the study stood out from the others as seeming desperately to need to be adopted, we considered that for the most part the difference between those foster children who were content with their status and those who were not lay in the attitudes of their local authority workers at the early stage when the question of permanence was discussed with them. When they talked to us about adoption and fostering, we heard the voices of their social workers coming through loud and clear, and the persuasive powers of the workers especially when a child is in 'limbo' were recognized by the workers themselves. As one project worker admitted, 'Mary was strongly programmed by us to accept what we were offering.'

Fourteen-year-old Mike, who had been abused by his first adoptive mother, was asked what he thought was the difference between adoption and fostering. He looked at us as if we must be stupid and said, 'Adoption's permanent.'

Our study suggests that, even if new families intend to adopt, adoption may, for a variety of reasons, emotional as well as practical, either not happen or not happen quickly. If this is likely to be the case, would it not be better in the early stages for workers to talk to children of a family where they will stay until they set up a home of their own rather than of an adoptive family? The dissatisfaction which some of the children felt on not being adopted was increased by their memories of local authority workers telling them that only adoption would give them the security of not being moved. Towards the end of the study, project workers were coming to feel that custodianship would have been a more appropriate status to aim for (had it then been available) for some of the older children. However, any status other than adoption was firmly established in the minds of some of the children as inferior. Yet in reality they *did* see the difference between short-term fostering and their own position, as this comment from a teenager foster child shows: 'Mum, have you ever considered fostering? You'd be good at it.'

The statutory roles of supervisor and decision-maker, whilst being deliberately played down in the interest of strengthening the growing authority of the new parents, were none the less taken seriously. Once the children had been placed, the local authority worker usually stopped seeing them on their own, and delegated her supervisory role to the project worker. Some workers did continue to visit the child, but only one of the children welcomed this. The project worker noted, 'Jean didn't need me. She needed her local authority social worker more. He was a sort of transitional object to her.' In contrast, Peter (aged 15) said of his local authority worker, 'She comes to see if there are any problems, if I'm happy here. She tries to tell me how to behave. She told me to apologize to dad. They'd think I was toadying about. We have a lot of arguments.'

Although the project workers tended not to see the children on their own, they looked for ways of discharging their supervisory obligations. One told us, 'I make sure I see him, watch him climbing his climbing frame – make sure I have a way of gauging whethr he is happy.'

In the majority of cases local authority and project workers referred to their decision-making role. Whilst they were clear that this was a task which they shared with the other members of the planning meeting and the review, it was none the less taken seriously, as the following comments by local authority workers show:

I think to myself, this is such an important decision. We are accountable to him for this. How is he going to feel in 15 years' time about it?

I feel it is my job, till he is placed, to prepare him and talk him through – to make the decisions with him. He has trusted me with information he hasn't trusted other people with. I have to make sure that the new family will be moving towards adoption.

It was, however, the decision-making role which the children disliked most, and whilst it was obviously important before a child was placed and until he was well settled, any reminders of this at later stages were most unwelcome. This was especially so of reviews, which were seen by the children we interviewed as at best irrelevant and a waste of time, and at worst an occasion for extreme anxiety which led to sleepless nights, disturbed behaviour and in one case a serious episode of delinquency.

SUMMARY

The main weakness we identified in the social work service concerned the 'welfare principle' and the requirement to 'ascertain the wishes and feelings of the child regarding the decision and give due consideration to them' (Children Act, 1975, sections 3 and 79). Sometimes social workers were too specific, or allowed a child to be too specific, about the sort of permanent placement to be found. As a result some children felt disappointed when not placed in their 'ideal homes', when, if promised something less specific, they would have been more satisfied with the 'good-enough' families eventually found for them. In several cases the least detrimental alternative involved placing children in homes where not all their needs were met. Sometimes we considered that some needs rightly took precedence over others, but at other times we considered that the social worker preparing the child was not listening hard enough to what was being said, or was deliberately assuming that she knew best. In some cases, if a different family or a different route to permanence had been chosen, children would not have needed to sabotage attempted linkings.

We have already observed that the style of social work with the children after placement was far removed from the high profile work recommended in *Foster Care: a guide to practice*' (DHSS, 1976) and by the recent DHSS *Study of the Boarding-out of Children* (1981). However, it was a style welcomed by parents and children, and we concluded that it helped the new family to function as a family. We would support Rowe and her colleagues (1984) and Triseliotis and Russell (1984) in their plea for recognition of a form of social work practice, and for new Boarding-Out Regulations for 'permanent' foster placements, that will encourage a sense of security rather than hinder it.

11

Conclusions and Recommendations

PERMANENT PLACEMENT RE-VIEWED

Since 1980 there have been many changes on the British child care scene. More residential units have closed, and family centres have come into fashion. The message that handicapped children can be successfully placed for adoption has been acted upon, and more such children are being placed earlier, before their difficulties have been compounded by long stays in residential care or hospital wards. This, and the fact that most local authorities have made their own arrangements for the adoption of children from care, may account for the fall in the numbers of really 'hard-to-place' children referred to the BAAF Exchange (down from 413 in 1983–4 to 273 in 1984–5: BAAF, 1985). Many of the 'children who wait' identified in the seventies have grown up and out of care, and the cumulative effect of these policy developments may prevent a similar backlog building up. Thanks largely to the 'Children in Need of Care' initiative of the DHSS and Economic and Social Research Council, we know much more about children coming into care and their subsequent care careers (Rowe et al., 1984; Fisher et al., 1986; Millham et al., 1986; Packman et al., 1986; Vernon and Fruin, 1986). They tend to be older on entering care, and, if anything, to come from families whose difficulties are even greater than used to be the case. Although there have been important initiatives in secondary prevention, with the growth of family centres, 'professional' fostering and intermediate treatment schemes, and progress has been made in the development of skills in working with children and families, primary prevention has all the appearance of being a lost cause with the increase in unemployment and reduced opportunities for day care, decent housing and adequate income maintenance. There is an increased likelihood that children will come into care through statutory routes, but Millham has found that, contrary to the general belief, this has not led to fewer moves in care or to better planning (Millham et al., 1985), whilst Packman shows that it diminishes parental satisfaction with the service offered (Packman et al., 1986). Several studies (Rowe et al., 1984; Fisher et al., 1986; Millham et al., 1985) have found that social work practice is still inadequate when it comes to helping parents and children to stay in contact. Millham and his colleagues have also shown that the majority of children coming into care will nevertheless eventually return to their natural families, or move into independent living situations. Of the 170 children aged under six on admission to care in the Dartington study (Millham et al., 1986, p. 187), only 24 were in long-term care two years later. This finding is important as a reminder that agencies, in initiating policies for the small numbers who need permanent family placement, must take care that these do not result in an inappropriate and unhelpful service to the far greater numbers who will eventually return to their parents and should be helped to do so as quickly as possible. This tendency was noted by Packman when she referred to the need 'to trace the unwanted and unforeseen consequences of change as well as its benefits' (Packman, 1981, p. 2). Has the move towards greater compulsion in child care in order to facilitate planning for permanence had the unforeseen consequence of a less appropriate and sensitive service to those who should go home? There are indications in these findings from recent research that this may be the case. The warning which these studies carry is that, if social work with parents and children at the time of reception or committal to care is not conducive to their staying in touch with one another, then some children will *unnecessarily* end up in long-term care and in need of permanent placement with substitute families. Many of these are likely to be older chidren, and in the category for whom permanent placement is most problematic.

It is against this background of changes in the population of children in care that the research into permanent placement has to be reviewed. Rowe and her colleagues (1984) and Triseliotis and Russell (1984) have reported on comparatively large samples of children placed in 'permanent' residential and foster care, and in adoptive homes, before the present enthusiasm for permanence took hold in Britain. Triseliotis and Russell's findings about the well-being of children placed for adoption when aged between two and ten give reason for optimism. 82 per cent of these adoptees when interviewed as young adults rated their growing-up experience positively – a rate no different from that for children adopted as babies. Rowe and her colleagues find enough positives in long-term foster care to recommend that it should remain a placement of choice for some, albeit a diminishing number of, children, but sound important notes of caution. It should be noted that these two studies are of children placed when the child care scene was very different from now. Principally, the children in their samples came into care when younger, and mostly their parents either consented to permanent placement with substitute families or had already ceased to play any significant role in their children's lives.

As yet there has been no British study to parallel the American research on permanence achieved by rehabilitation with natural families. Nor, indeed, are there any specialist projects aiming to achieve permanence by a variety of routes of which return to natural families is one.

Finally, in this brief review of child care research, we turn to studies of children placed more recently with permanent substitute families. Wolkind and Kozaruk (1986) followed up 84 children 'with medical difficulties' placed through the ARE between 1974 and 1978 (average age at placement three years). Three years after placement, 95 per cent were still with their new families. They found that the degree of handicap was not related to outcome. 'The factor that did predict behavioural problems was where the child had been prior to placement. Children adopted from children's homes were the ones most likely to show this type of disorder' (Wolkind and Kozaruk, 1983, p. 34). Other studies have involved smaller numbers mostly placed by individual agencies. Reich and Lewis (1986) describe 69 children placed by Parents for Children, and Macaskill (1985a) looks at the post-placement needs of 37 of the most complex placements made by the same agency. The annual reports of Parents for Children show that 89 children were placed in the first eight years and that 15 per cent were disrupted. In a separate study, Macaskill (1985b) followed up 23 mentally handicapped children and their new adoptive families. Wedge (1986) provides us with the only independent evaluation of local authority permanency units, and finds that, despite initial tensions, professional and administrative, 'in-house' specialist provision can operate successfully and find homes for 'hard-to-place' children who would otherwise be stuck in the care system.

Practitioners have also described and evaluated their own work, as in the case of Parents for Children (Sawbridge, 1983; Argent, 1984), Barnardo's Cambridge Cottage Project (Fratter et al., 1982) and Barnado's New Families Project (Kerrane et al., 1981; Lindsay-Smith and Price, 1980). Such accounts, along with the annual reports of these and other pioneering family finding agencies, are rich sources of fact and 'practice wisdom'. Most of these agencies took part in a DHSS-sponsored workshop (Wedge and Thoburn, 1986) where there was substantial agreement about conclusions to be drawn from the research. All set out primarily to consider whether permanent placement for 'hard-to-place' children works; all decided that it did but that the 'hard-to-place' category needed to be further subdivided. For instance, for younger handicapped children, even those with very severe handicaps, there is a high probability of successful placement with adoptive families. The difficulty lies in findings the right family as quickly as possible, and in the fact that the right family may well be unconventional and not fit what local authority adoption panels usually see as 'suitable'. This same applies also to young black children, for whom black families are now being sought. Once the child has been placed, the help needed tends to be mainly of a practical and resource nature.

Turning to older children, although findings are encouraging, researchers and practitioners agree that the really 'hard-to-place' children are likely to be older, and to have educational or behaviour problems, which may be compounded by institutionalization. They are also likely to have ambivalent relationships with birth parents but to be reluctant to lose all contact with them, siblings or other relatives. They are, then, precisely the kind of children which the research studies mentioned above have identified as 'typical' children in care. For these youngsters the research shows that the heady days of 'no child is unadoptable' are over. A more accurate conclusion from the studies would be that no *category* of child is unadoptable, but, for a proportion of *individuals* who need permanent placement, adoption will be either inappropriate or impracticable. Even those agencies which always place with adoption in mind have found that some new parents never reach the stage when it feels right to make the child legally a part of their family, even though continuing to be parents in every other sense. Macaskill (1985a), who looked carefully into this when studying placements which were running into difficulties, found no evidence to support the commonly held view that 'the security of adoption would ameliorate difficulties in problematic placements. I searched in vain through ensuing histories of children for any evidence to validate this belief.' Lahti (1982), in one of the American large-scale studies, concluded that it was the 'sense of permanence' which was important, and that this was not necessarily related to legal status.

Another widely held view is that termination of contact with members of the birth family, even for older children, should precede introduction to a new family. There is nothing in the various studies either to confirm or to contradict this view. A substantial minority of the children were successfully placed without parental consent, with access terminated against the wishes of parents and sometimes of the children themselves. However, before finally confirming these placements as successful, one will need to know how the children fare in adolescene. The CWAH study and that of Fratter and colleagues (1982) show that those children who did remain in contact with members of their birth families after placement were doing as well as comparable children whose access was terminated. From our own study we concluded that some children will not allow themselves to be placed with substitute families if termination of contact with members of the natural family is a prerequisite of placement.

RECOMMENDATIONS

Our recommendations are based not only on our own interpretation of facts and events, but also on the views of those research colleagues and other specialists who spent many hours talking with us about permanent placement and about our findings; the views of the social workers we interviewed for the study; and, most importantly, the views of the children themselves and members of their new families. Many points of detail have been made in preceding chapters and we concentrate here on four main issues.

Routes to permanence

The type of 'permanence' should depend on the needs of the child, and no one route should be seen as intrinsically preferable to another. In Britian, the 'adoption without contact' route has been shown to be successful for a wider range of children than was previously thought possible, and a particularly appropriate and skilful model of social work practice has evolved. Research has indicated, and practitioners have discovered for themselves, that adoption or loss of parental contact is not appropriate for some of the children referred, especially some of the older children, and practitioners have found that the skills developed for settling children in new families can be equally appropriate and successful in resettling children with natural families. To date, this sort of work has been a by-product of inappropriate referrals. There is a need now to devote the same skills and resources to finding permanence through other routes – both 'inclusive' permanence, whether through adoption, custodianship or long-term foster care, and permanence achieved through return to natural families. To aid this process, 'demonstration' projects should be funded in the statutory and voluntary sectors and carefully researched.

It could be argued that such developments might confuse the message about the need to take clear if difficult decisions, and that permanence owes its success to the clarity of its message. On the other hand, Parker (1985) has argued that diversity and at times uncertainty have to be accepted as part of planning, if the needs of individual children are to be met. Indeed, it could be that the quest for certainty is at times the enemy of the quest for permanence, in that it can lead to a rigidity which will prevent some childen from making the choice.

Social work with natural parents

The willingness to look at a range of permanence options will in itself lead to improvements in the service to natural parents of children for whom return home is not possible. The requirements in the Adoption Agencies Regulations to discuss with parents all the alternatives to adoption and to inform the court of their views should, if more than lip service is to be paid to them, lead to a better service, as will the *Code of Practice on Access to Children in Care* (DHSS, 1983).

The aim of 'inclusive' permanence will be greatly helped by accepting only voluntary contributions from the parents of children in permanent foster care or those whose children are placed with custodians to whom an allowance is paid. Our study showed that 'inclusive' permanence is both worthwhile and potentially stressful, and it is as well to avoid the extra stress of conflict over payments not arriving or arriving late. There was worrying evidence of pressure on parents to consent to adoption in order to end the burden on their own new families of contributing to the cost of the child in care. This hardly seems an appropriate reason for a child to lose all contact with a significant person from the past who, albeit no longer able to offer permanent care, is willing to accept that it is in the child's interest to become a part of someone else's family.

Social work with new families

The CWAH social workers followed closely a model of practice for the recruitment, preparation and support of new families which has been more than adequately described elsewhere (Sawbridge, 1983; Argent, 1984). New parents, their own children and the children joining them appreciated this 'at one remove' style of work, which placed the main authority and helping role with the parents. This consumer satisfaction has to be set against the risk that problems in the placement may go undetected if the child is not offered a 'one-to-one' relationship with a social worker. Against this view it can be argued that, if one tries to ride two horses at once, one risks getting badly hurt by falling through the gap. If one has decided to ride the 'permanent new family' horse, it would seem wise, even though some risk is involved, to give that horse every chance of arriving at its destination. A heavy emphasis on the authority of the social worker is likely to hinder the ability of the new family to 'knit together' and may so promote the very insecurity which permanent placement is meant to counteract. The critical stage is the matching of the child's needs with what the family has to offer. If it isn't right at this stage, no amount of back-seat driving will make it right. It will only succeed in making everybody, especially the child, more nervous and insecure. Hence, for children in 'permanent' care with substitute families, we recommend a form of social work practice different from the high profile work which is essential when children are in temporary or 'treatment' placements, and that this should be allowed for in Boarding-Out Regulations and review procedures.

The severe difficulties encountered by a small minority of the new families have led to serious thought being given to post-placement support. Macaskill (1985a) concludes that the usual sources of support available in the community are not seen by substitute families as appropriate to their needs. On the other hand, one of our conclusions was that the project worker for the family was usually not the best person to offer therapy if severe stress affected family functioning. It would appear from our own and Macaskill's study that the critical time will be months or years after placement. Post-adoption support services need to be set up which build on the knowledge now available.

Service delivery

Placing children with permanent new families demands creativity, knowledge, skill, a steady nerve in the face of risk-taking, a high level of administrative efficiency and an impeccable sense of timing. It is therefore time-consuming and expensive. If local authorities espouse the philosophy of permanence without willing the means to do the work properly, they risk bringing 'permanence' into disrepute, and it will become just another discarded social work fashion.

Reviews of consumer research usually note that most clients of personal social services tend to differentiate between the social worker and the agency. The social worker is more often that not valued, whilst the agency is rarely seen as helpful. In permanent placements projects, as this study and others in the same area have shown, the consumers value the workers and their agencies equally. It is this degree of consumer satisfaction, from new families and from referring social workers, and a 'success' rate which compares very favourably with long-term placements of similar children made by local authorities, which leads us to recommend that social services departments should set up small units of specialist workers if they really intend to offer the benefits of permanence to children in long-term care. Whether these units should work only towards permanent placement with new families or should also take rehabilitation into their brief is an open question. There is scope here for experimentation, and Wedge (1986), in describing the work of the Essex family-finders, gives some clues about the ways in which such units might develop, and find an appropriate role within their parent social services departments. The problems of inter-agency social work, we are well aware, are as likely to be present in relations between separate sections of large departments, and to overcome them will require equally sensitive, efficient and time-consuming work. It was the realization that large and bureaucratic organizations have serious weaknesses when it comes to parenting children in long-term care which gave rise to the permanence movement. Ways therefore have to be found both to prevent these same weaknesses from impeding the risk-taking inherent in finding permanent substitute families, and also to provide the settings in which all of those taking the risks – social workers, new families and children themselves – feel most comfortable and confident.

Postscript

The little prince went away to look again at the roses.

'You are not at all like my rose,' he said. 'As yet you are nothing. No one has tamed you, and you have tamed no one. You are like my fox when I first knew him. He was only a fox like a hundred thousand other foxes. But I have made him my friend, and now he is unique in all the world.'

And the roses were very much embarrassed.

'You are beautiful, but you are empty,' he went on. 'One could not die for you. To be sure, an ordinary passer-by would think that my rose looked just like you – the rose that belongs to me. But in herself alone she is more important than all the hundreds of you other roses: because it is she that I have watered; because it is she that I have put under the glass globe; because it is she that I have sheltered behind the screen; because it is for her that I have killed the caterpillars (except the two or three that we saved to become butterflies); because it is she that I have listened to when she grumbled, or boasted, or even sometimes when she said nothing. Because she is *my* rose.' . . .

'I am responsible for my rose,' the little prince repeated, so that he would be sure to remember.

(Saint-Exupéry, The Little Prince*)*

We have followed the children in their search for parents who would be 'unique' to them and to whom they would be 'unique'. But the story of the little prince provides an appropriate analogy also for the workers who undertook the risky and sometimes painful task of finding permanent families for children who had already been hurt, and could, by their actions, be hurt again. We have traced their enterprise through three particularly 'heady' years. The project was born out of the 'No Child is Unadoptable' (Churchill, 1979) era, and as it developed and matured acquired the self-confidence that comes from success and increasing knowledge. If we had taken our cases from those referred in the third and fourth years, the success rate would have been even higher, as workers came to recognize more clearly the sort of children for whom permanent placement with new families was appropriate.

When we started the research we had more reservations than we now have about this work. We have been agreeably surprised by the apparent ease with which the younger children, despite the difficulties which made them 'hard-to-place', have fitted into their new families, and at the pleasure they have brought. We have picked out as a major theme the placement of older children who still have ties with members of their birth families, and where the desirability or otherwise of continued contact is problematic. This was one of the main questions we set out to explore, in the belief that that right balance between past and future is a major unresolved issue which must be worked through if more children in care are to be offered secure family placements and allow themselves to accept them. They must not be forgotten in the pursuit of more successful, less costly or less risky work. They need secure family placement, and the CWAH has shown that they can be placed. But for each the route to permanence – the balance between past and future – will be different. Some, like the little prince, will seek permanence by returning to what they know – by making the most of the less than perfect relationships they have with their natural parents. Others will move on, giving up the past to a greater or lesser extent, and at a faster or slower pace, in the quest for new and lasting relationships.

Practice wisdom such as we have described, and the pointers which we and others have given about effective social work, should help with this skilled and sometimes painful work. But the route to permanence must be unique to each child. For each and every case the 'chemistry' – the relationship between the child and those he loved in the past, and those he may come to love in the future – will be different.

'Goodbye,' he said.

'Goodbye,' said the fox. 'And now here is my secret, a very simple secret: it is only with the heart that one can see rightly: what is essential is invisible to the eye.'

'What is essential is invisible to the eye,' the little prince repeated so that he would be sure to remember.

'It is the time you have wasted for your rose that makes your rose so important.'

'It is the time I have wasted for my rose –', said the little prince, so that he would be sure to remember.

(*Saint-Exupéry*, The Little Prince)

Bibliography

Adock, M. 1980: The right to permanent placement. *Adoption and Fostering*, 4 (1), 21–4.

Adcock, M. and Lawrence, L. 1975: Lack of planning – lack of care. *Concern* (National Children's Bureau), 16.

Adcock, M. and White, R. (eds) 1980: *Terminating Parental Contact*. London: ABAFA.

Adoption Resource Exchange 1980: *Working Together: a guide to the policy and practice of inter-agency adoption placements*. London: ARE.

Aldgate, J. 1980: Identification of factors which influence length of stay in care. In J. P. Triseliotis, *New Developments in Foster Care and Adoption*, London: Routledge and Kegan Paul.

Argent, H. 1984: *Find Me a Family*. London: Souvenir Press.

Association of British Adoption and Fostering Agencies (1977): *Planning for Children in Long Term Care*. London: ABAFA.

Bacon, R. and Rowe, J. 1978: *The Use and Misuse of Resources*. London: ABAFA.

Barclay Committee 1982: *Social Workers: their role and tasks*. London: Bedford Square Press.

Berridge, D. 1985: *Children's Homes*. Oxford: Basil Blackwell.

Bowlby, J. 1951: *Maternal Care and Mental Health*. Geneva: World Health Organization.

—— 1971: *Attachment and Loss*. Harmondsworth: Penguin.

—— 1977: The making and breaking of affectional bonds. *British Journal of Psychiatry*, 130, 201–10.

British Agencies for Adoption and Fostering 1985: *Annual Review 1984/5*. London: BAAF.

British Association of Social Workers 1982: *Guidelines for Practice in Family Placement*. Birmingham: BASW.

Burgoyne, J. and Clark, D. 1981: Parenting in stepfamilies. In R. Chester (ed.), *Changing Patterns in Child-bearing and Child-rearing*, London: Academic Press.

—— 1982: Family reconstitution. In Family Research Committee (eds), *Families in Britain*, London: Routledge and Kegan Paul.

Central Council for Education and Training in Social Work 1978: *Good Enough Parenting.* London: HMSO.

Children's Society 1984: *The Child Wants a Home – the fourth year.* Norwich: Children's Society.

The Child Wants a Home 1980: *Introductory Booklet.* Norwich: Children's Society.

Churchill, S. R. 1979: *No Child is Unadoptable.* Beverley Hills, Calif.: Sage.

Clark, B. 1977: A cause of concern – child care policy and practice. *Social Work Today*, 8 (43), 7–10.

Clark, D. 1982: Restarting a family: having children in second marriages. In R. Chester (ed.), *Children and Marriage*, Hull: Barmarick.

Cooper, J. 1978: *Patterns of Family Placement.* London: National Children's Bureau.

Crowley, M. 1982: *Preparation for Foster Care Practice.* Norwich: University of East Anglia Social Work Monographs.

Curtis, P. 1983: Involving children in the placement process. *Adoption and Fostering*, 7 (1), 45–7.

Department of Health and Social Security 1976: *Foster Care: a guide to practice.* London: HMSO.

—— 1981: *A Study of the Boarding-out of Children*, London: HMSO.

—— 1983: *Code of Practice on Access to Children in Care.* London: HMSO.

—— 1984: *Report of the House of Commons Social Services Committee.* London: HMSO.

Donley, K. 1975: *Opening New Doors.* London: ABAA.

Erikson, E. H. 1965: *Identity, Youth and Crisis.* London: Hogarth Press.

—— 1983: *Childhood and Society.* London: Hogarth Press.

Fahlberg, V. 1981: *Helping Children When They Must Move.* London: BAAF.

Fallon, M., McKenna, M., Waring, P., Wilson, G., Thom, M. and Giltinan, D. 1983: Placing adolescents in families. *Adoption and Fostering*, 7 (4), 43–6.

Family Rights Group 1982: *Accountability in Social Work.* London: Family Rights Group.

Fanshel, D. and Shinn, E. B. 1978: *Children in Foster Care – A Longitudinal Study.* New York: Columbia University Press.

Fein, E., Maluccio, A. N., Hamilton, V. J., Ward, D. E. 1983: After foster care: permanency planning for children. *Child Welfare*, 62 (6), 486–567.

Fisher, M., Marsh, P. Phillips, D., Sainsbury, E. E. 1986: *In and Out of Care. The Experience of Children, Parents and Social Workers*, London: Batsford/BAAF.

Fitzgerald, J. 1977: Making decisions. *Adoption and Fostering*, 1 (3), 14–19.

—— 1983: *Understanding Disruption.* London: BAAF.

Fitzgerald, J., Murcer, B. and Murcer, B. 1982: *Building New Families through Adoption and Fostering*. Oxford: Basil Blackwell.

Fox, L. M. 1982: Two value positions in recent child care law and practice. *British Journal of Social Work*, 12 (3), 265–90.

Fratter, J., Newton, D. and Shinegold, D. 1982: *Cambridge Cottage Pre-Fostering and Adoption Unit*. Barkingside, Essex: Barnardo Social Work Papers no. 16.

Gath, A. 1983: Mentally retarded children in substitute and natural families. *Adoption and Fostering*, 7 (1), 35–40.

George, V. 1970: *Foster Care*. London: Routledge and Kegan Paul.

Gill, O. and Jackson, B. 1982: *Adoption and Race*. London: Batsford.

Goldstein, J., Freud, A. and Solnit, A. 1973: *Beyond the Best Interests of the Child*. New York: Free Press.

Harlow Parents' Aid 1982: *Guide for Parents with Children in Care*. Harlow: Parents' Aid.

Hazel, N. 1981: *A Bridge to Independence*. Oxford: Basil Blackwell.

Hipgrave, T. 1983: Adolescence and fostering. *Adoption and Fostering*, 7 (4), 39–43.

Holman, B. 1981: *Kids at the Door*. Oxford: Basil Blackwell.

—— 1983: *Resourceful Friends*. London: Children's Society.

Holman, R. 1975: The place of fostering in social work. *British Journal of Social Work*, 5 (1), 3–29.

——1976: *Inequality in Child Care*. London: Child Poverty Action Group.

Hussell, C. and Monaghan, B. 1982: Child care planning in Lambeth. *Adoption and Fostering*, 6 (2), 21–5.

James, G. 1979: The child centred approach to children in care. In D. Brandon and B. Jordan (eds), *Creative Social Work*. Oxford: Basil Blackwell.

James, M. 1980: Home-finding for children with special needs. In J. P. Triseliotis (ed.), *New Developments in Foster Care and Adoption*, London: Routledge and Kegan Paul.

Jenkins, S. and Norman, E. 1972: *Filial Deprivation and Foster Care*. New York: Columbia University Press.

Jewett, C. L. 1978: *Adopting the Older Child*. Cambridge, Mass.: Harvard Common Press.

—— 1984: *Helping Children Cope with Separation and Loss*. London: Batsford.

Jones, M. A., Neuman, R. and Shyne, A. 1976: *A Second Chance for Families*. New York: Child Welfare League of America.

Jordan, B. 1981: Prevention. *Adoption and Fostering*, 5 (3), 20–2.

Kadushin, A. 1970: *Adopting Older Children*. New York: Columbia University Press.

Kadushin, A. and Seidl, F. W. 1971: Adoption failure: a social work post mortem. *Social Work*, 16 (3).

Kelly, G. 1981: The lost cord. *Social Work Today*, 13 (12), 7–9.

Kerrane, A., Hunter, A. and Lane, M. 1981: *Adopting Older and Handicapped Children*. Barkingside, Essex: Barnardo's Social Work Paper no. 14.

Lahti, J. 1982: A follow-up study of foster children in permanent placements. *Social Service Review* (University of Chicago), 556–71.

Lambert, L. and Streather, J. 1980: *Children in Changing Families*. London: Macmillan.

Lightbown, C. 1979: Life story books. *Adoption and Fostering*, 3 (3), 9–15.

Lindsay-Smith, C. and Price, E. 1980: *Barnardo's New Families Project – Glasgow: the first two years*. Barkingside, Essex: Barnardo's Social Work Papers no. 13.

Littner, N. 1960: The child's need to repeat his past: some implications for placement. *Social Services Review*, 34 (2), 128–48.

Lowenfeld, M. 1979: *The World Technique*. London: Allen and Unwin.

Lynch, M. and Roberts J. 1982: *Consequences of Child Abuse*. London: Academic Press.

Macaskill, C. 1985a: Post-adoption support: is it essential? *Adoption and Fostering*, 9 (1) and (2).

—— 1985b: *Against the Odds. Adopting mentally handicapped children*. London: BAAF.

McKay, M. 1980: Planning for permanent placement. *Adoption and Fostering*, 4 (1), 19–21.

Maluccio, A. N., Fein, E., Hamilton, J., Klier, J. L. and Ward, D. 1980: Beyond permanency planning. *Child Welfare*, 59, 515–30.

Maluccio, A. N. and Fein, E. 1983: Permanency planning: a redefinition. *Child Welfare*, 62 (3), 195–201.

Maluccio, A. and Sinanoglu, P. A. 1981: *The Challenge of Partnership: working with parents of children in foster care*. New York: Child Welfare League of America.

Mayer, J. and Timms, N. 1970: *The Client Speaks*. London: Routledge and Kegan Paul.

Millham, S., Bullock, R., Hosie, K. and Haak, M. 1986: *Children Lost in Care: The family contact of children in care*. Farnborough: Gower.

Morris, C. 1984: *The Permanency Principle in Child Care Social Work*. Norwich: University of East Anglia Social Work Monographs.

National Foster Care Association 1983: *Memorandum to the House of Commons Social Services Committee*. London: National Foster Care Association.

Packman, J. 1981: *The Child's Generation*, 2nd edn. Oxford: Basil Blackwell.

—— , Randall, J. and Jacques, N. 1986: *Who needs care? Social Work Decisions about Children*. Oxford: Basil Blackwell.

Parker, R. A. 1980: *Caring for Separated Children*. London: Macmillan.

—— 1985: Planning into practice. *Adoption and Fostering*, 9 (4).

Phelan, J. 1983: *Family Centres: a study*. London: Children's Society.

Raynor, L. 1970: *Adoption of Non-white Children*. London: Allen and Unwin.

Rees, S. 1978: *Social Work Face to Face: clients' and social workers' perceptions of the content and outcome of their meetings*. London: E. Arnold.

Rees, S. and Wallace, A. 1982: *Verdicts on Social Work*. London: E. Arnold.

Reich, D. and Lewis, J. 1986: Placement by Parents for children. In P. Wedge and J. Thoburn (eds), *The Hard to Place Experience*, London: BAAF.

Rimmer, L. 1983: *Families in Focus: marriage, divorce and family patterns*. London: Study Commission on the Family.

Robertson, J. and Robertson, J. 1977: The psychological parent. *Adoption and Fostering*, 1 (1), 19–22.

Rowe, J. 1977: Fostering in the seventies. *Adoption and Fostering*, 1 (4), 15–20.

—— 1983: *Fostering in the Eighties*. London: BAAF.

Rowe, J., Cain, H., Hundleby, M. and Keane, A. 1984: *Long-term Foster Care*. London: Batsford/BAAF.

Rowe, J. and Lambert, L. 1973: *Children who Wait*. London: ABAA.

Rutter, M. 1972: *Maternal Deprivation Reassessed*. Harmondsworth: Penguin.

—— 1975: Attainment and adjustment in two geographical areas. *British Journal of Psychiatry*, 125, 493–509.

Sainsbury, E. 1975: *Social Work with Families*. London: Routledge and Kegan Paul.

Sainsbury, E., Nixon, S. and Philips, D. 1982: *Social Work in Focus*. London: Routledge and Kegan Paul.

Saint-Exupéry, A. de 1945: *The Little Prince*. London: Piccolo.

Sawbridge, P. 1980: Seeking new parents: a decade of development. In J. P. Triseliotis (ed.), *New Developments in Foster Care and Adoption*, London: Routledge and Kegan Paul.

—— 1981: Working together. *Adoption and Fostering*, 4 (1), 31–5.

—— 1983: *Parents for Children*. London: BAAF.

Sawbridge, P. and Carriline, M. 1978: Social work tasks in relation to placing children in new families. In Central Council for Education and Training in Social Work, *Good Enough Parenting*, London: CCETSW.

Shaw, I. 1975: Consumer opinion and social policy. *Journal of Social Policy*, 5 (1), 19–32.

Shaw, M. and Hipgrave, T. 1983: *Specialist Fostering*. London: Batsford/BAAF.

Sherman, E., Neuman, R. and Shyne, A. 1973: *Children Adrift in Foster Care*. New York: Child Welfare League of America.

Smith, C. R. 1984: *Adoption and Fostering: why and how*, London, Macmillan.

Stein, T. J., Gambrill, E. D. and Wiltse, K. T. 1978: *Children in Foster Homes: achieving continuity of care*. New York: Praeger.

Stevenson, O. 1980: Family problems and patterns in the 1980s. *Adoption and Fostering*, 4 (2), 20–4.

Stevenson, O. and Parsloe, P. 1978: *Social Service Teams: the practitioner's view*. London: HMSO.

Tizard, B. 1977: *Adoption, a Second Chance*. London: Open Books.

Thoburn, J. 1980: *Captive Clients*. London: Routledge and Kegan Paul.

Thoburn, J., Murdoch, A. and O'Brien, A. 1985: *A Study of Permanent Family Placement of Children in Care who Have Special Needs. A report to the DHSS*. Norwich: University of East Anglia.

Thorpe, R. 1980: The experience of parents and children living apart: implications and guidelines for practice. In J. P. Triseliotis (ed.), *New Developments in Foster Care and Adoption*, London: Routledge and Kegan Paul.

Triseliotis, J. P. 1983: Identity and security in adoption and long-term fostering. *Adoption and Fostering*, 7 (1), 22–31.

—— (ed.) 1980: *New Developments in Foster Care and Adoption*. London: Routledge and Kegan Paul.

Triseliotis, J. P. and Russell, J. 1984: *Hard to Place: the outcomes of adoption and residential care*. London: Heinemann and Gower.

Vernon, J. and Fruin, D. 1986: *In Care: a study of social work decision-making*. London: National Children's Bureau.

Wedge, P. 1986: Family finding in Essex. In P. Wedge and J. Thoburn, *The Hard to Place Experience*, London: BAAF.

Wedge, P. and Thoburn, J. (eds) 1986: *The Hard to Place Experience*. London: BAAF.

Wilcox, K. and Allen, M. 1983: Intermediate fostering schemes in Lambeth. *Adoption and Fostering*, 7 (4), 17–19.

Winnicott, D. W. 1965: *The Family and Individual Development*. London: Tavistock.

Wolkind, S. 1974: The components of affectionless psychopathy in institutionalized children. *Journal of Child Psychology and Psychiatry*, 15, 215.

Wolkind, S. and Kozaruk, A. 1983: The adoption of children with medical handicap. *Adoption and Fostering*, 7 (1), 32–5.

—— 1986: Placement of children with medical difficulties. In P. Wedge and J. Thoburn (eds), *The Hard to Place Experience*, London: BAAF.

Index